AF555993

In his book *Dark Secrets*, Iqbal Chand Malhotra has revealed the unknown interplay of forces in the great game. A strategist would learn from here, the chessboard setting for the future, with special reference to India. One thing that catches my attention is how the buffer players cause subtle interference and create new claims altering the contour of maps.

—Lieutenant General P.J.S. Pannu PVSM, AVSM, VSM,
former Deputy Chief IDS,
former 14 Corps Commander (Ladakh),
former DG Infantry Indian Army

A gripping and action-packed account of Kashmir at the centre of the 'great game' between Britain and Russia from the end of the 19th century to 1948. Iqbal has used literary license to plug gaps left by missing records to write a work of 'creative non-fiction' which makes for a compelling read. The 'great game' was initiated through diplomatic intrigues in Kashgar. For a time, to the utter consternation of the British, the better resourced Russians nearly reached south towards Gilgit, but the competition was resolved in the old fashioned way through the intercession of the two monarchs—Queen Victoria, who was the grandmother of the Russian Tsar. The result was the Anglo Russian Convention of 1907. Consequently, the British seized control of Gilgit, Nagar and Hunza, and built roads through these territories. Iqbal gives a detailed account of how the British manipulated royal succession in Kashmir and severely circumscribed the powers of Maharaja Pratap Singh and his successor Maharaja Hari Singh. He traces the growth of popular movements in Kashmir in the 1930s including the secular-communal divide between Sheikh Abdullah and the Mirwaiz. Iqbal avers that Mountbatten and British military leaders manipulated Nehru into making decisions that led to a stalemate in Kashmir in 1948. The reason—and this is the central thesis of the book—was the British interest in spying on the Soviet nuclear programme from top-secret bases in Kashmir, Punjab and NWFP after the Americans denied them access to the results and secrets of the US nuclear programme. This thesis and some interesting subplots in the narrative will no doubt stoke controversy, for example, Bose, writes Iqbal, did not die in the plane crash in Taipei but escaped to Russia and tried to re-enter India from the NWFP. All in all, a compelling read!

—Biren Nanda,
former Ambassador to Indonesia and ASEAN,
former High Commissioner to Australia

Iqbal Chand Malhotra's book takes us on an exciting exploration of the secret world that shaped India's north-western frontier and Kashmir. It examines the contours of the last great game between Imperial Russia and Great Britain during the 19th and early 20th centuries. Significantly, it points out how the Soviet control of Sinkiang influenced not only the politics of the British, but ultimately, impacted the partition of

India and the Sino-Indian relationship up to the present. Well-researched, with new material to support his fluent narrative, the imaginative re-reading of certain facts lends new depth and understanding to our study of the geopolitics and history of that region.

—Professor Dr Ravni Thakur,
Head of Department, East Asian Studies,
University of Delhi

DARK SECRETS

DARK SECRETS

Politics, Intrigue and Proxy Wars in Kashmir

Iqbal Chand Malhotra

B L O O M S B U R Y
NEW DELHI • LONDON • OXFORD • NEW YORK • SYDNEY

BLOOMSBURY INDIA
Bloomsbury Publishing India Pvt. Ltd
Second Floor, LSC Building No. 4, DDA Complex, Pocket C – 6 & 7,
Vasant Kunj, New Delhi, 110070

BLOOMSBURY, BLOOMSBURY INDIA and the Diana logo
are trademarks of Bloomsbury Publishing Plc

First published in India 2021
This edition published 2024

ISBN: PB: 978-93-56409-73-6; eBook: 978-93-54355-45-5
2 4 6 8 10 9 7 5 3 1

Typeset in Fournier MT Std by Manipal Technologies Limited
Printed and bound in India by Thomson Press India Ltd

CONTENTS

LIST OF IMAGES

LIST OF ABBREVIATIONS

AFOAT	Air Force Office-Atomic Testing
CCP	Chinese Communist Party
CIA	Central Intelligence Agency
C-in-C	Commander-in-Chief
CPC	Communist Party of China
CPI	Communist Party of India
CPPCC	Chinese People's Political Consultative Conference
DSO	Distinguished Service Order
FIU	Field Intelligence Unit
GHQ	General Headquarters
GMT	Greenwich Mean Time
GOC	General Officer Commanding
GRU	Main Intelligence Directorate of the Red Army
HQ	HQ
HUMINT	Human Intelligence
IAF	Indian Air Force
IB	Intelligence Bureau
ICS	Indian Civil Service
IG	Inspector General
INA	Indian National Army
IPS	Indian Political Service
KGB	Komitet Gosudarstvennoy Bezopasnosti (Committee for State Security)

KMT	Kuomintang Party of China
KPD	Communist Party of Germany
LAC	Line of Actual Control
LoC	Line of Control
MBE	Member of British Empire
MC	Military Cross
MI6	Foreign Intelligence Service of the UK
NKVD	People's Commissariat for Internal Affairs (the Soviet secret service agency)
NSDAP/AO	Nazi Party/Foreign Organisation
NSF&DF	National Socialist Women's League
NWFP	North-West Frontier Province
OGPU	Joint State Political Directorate under the Council of People's Commissars of the USSR
OKW	Oberkommando der Wehrmacht or the High Command of the Nazi German Armed Forces
PLA	People's Liberation Army
POK	Pakistan Occupied Kashmir
POW	Prisoner of War
PRC	People's Republic of China
PST	Pakistan Standard Time
RAF	Royal Air Force
RIAF	Royal Indian Air Force
RPAF	Royal Pakistan Air Force
RU	Registration Directorate (Registrupravlenie)
SIGINT	Signals Intelligence
SS	Schutzstaffel or Paramilitary in Nazi Germany

TAL	Tube Alloys Liaison/Technical Atomic Liaison
TASS	Telegrafnoje Agentstvo Sovietskovo Soïuza (Soviet news agency)
TNT	Trinitrotoluene
UNCIP	United Nations Commission for India and Pakistan
USAAF	United States Army Air Forces
USAF	United States Air Force
VC	Victoria Cross

Introduction

This book is a work of creative non-fiction. The genre of creative non-fiction enables the author to circumvent the limitations of recorded data surrounding certain events and use literary license to plug the gaps, join the dots and, if lucky, come up with an internally consistent and compelling story.

I started researching on Kashmir in 2014 when Discovery Channel commissioned me to make a film on the Line of Control (LoC). I delved deeper into the subject a year later when the channel commissioned me again to make a film on the Siachen Glacier. Thereafter, in 2017, Times Now commissioned me to produce a series of six one-hour films called *The Story of Kashmir*. My good friend Maroof Raza was the subject expert in each of these projects.

I remember, after handing over the films to Times Now in 2018, I told Maroof that there was much, much more to the story of Kashmir than what was portrayed in the just-completed series. For one, lack of funds rendered access to archival footage from sources like British Pathe and British Movietone impossible, which greatly hampered the prospect of harnessing the power of storytelling. Further, the inability to recreate dramatic scenes and events with actors put a cap on the potential of the series. Maroof, however, always responded with solutions rather than cut a despairing figure.

Maroof also helped open new avenues for collaboration. Towards the end of 2018, he introduced me to a publisher at Bloomsbury who, to my utter surprise, commissioned Maroof and me to co-author *Kashmir's Untold Story: Declassified*. I must confess that I thoroughly enjoyed the process of writing the book. While researching for the book, some interesting facts were brought to light. I discovered that conventional academic historians largely followed recorded history and reinterpret it at best. They ignored parallel events that were unfolding in the same environment that they were writing about. These parallel events when juxtaposed against recorded events reveal patterns that needed to be reassembled to provide fresh coherence to events that had already transpired and been recorded conventionally.

The existing picture in many cases is like an eye that sees blurred visuals because of a layer of cataract over it. This blurred reality is very often deliberately nudged into a new clarity that is sold to the viewer as the original 'true' reality. The viewer invariably accepts it because the seller of this reality is extremely accomplished in the art of selling. Especially when the seller is a popular politician, the viewer lets himself or herself be led into believing the distorted or incomplete reality as the prevailing truth. Conventional recorders of contemporary and later historical events give truth to this lie by reinterpreting and reinforcing it without pondering over why they are uncomfortable in stretching their vision to discover newer patterns and still newer shades of the truth.

As for me, I have instead taken on the role of a quantum field observer who does not choose an option to collapse into reality but follows a pattern and lets the pattern collapse into reality as it was when it was unfolding in real-time.

After completing the book I co-authored with Maroof, I looked back at this quantum field of multiple events around Kashmir; I could still see other patterns that seemed more complex and enticing than the patterns that we had discovered and written about.

I kept this alternate reality close to my chest, and it evolved into a book called *Red Fear: The China Threat*, which was authored by me and published by Bloomsbury in 2020. But I was still dissatisfied with the Kashmir story as something about it continued to bother me. So, I teamed up with Maroof once again and we wrote a revised edition of our book that was first published in 2019. The new version was published as a revised and updated edition in January 2021. This changed the story of Kashmir as it brought a new pattern within the ambit of the story.

However, I was still not satisfied.

To explain my dissatisfaction, I am tempted to return to my analogy of quantum mechanics; I am reproducing here perhaps the most popular interpretation of quantum theory by the famous physicist Werner Heisenberg:

> Of course, the introduction of the observer must not be misunderstood to imply that some kind of subjective features are to be brought into the description of nature. The observer has, rather, only the function of registering decisions, i.e., processes in space and

> time, and it does not matter whether the observer is an apparatus or a human being; but the registration, i.e., the transition from the 'possible' to the 'actual,' is absolutely necessary here and cannot be omitted from the interpretation of quantum theory.

What I then proceeded to do was replace the concept of 'observer' in quantum theory with 'forensic historian' in my theory of Kashmir. The purpose of the forensic historian then is to look for patterns and reconstruct a new picture by weaving in the hitherto ignored reality into the present reality to give birth to a new 'actual', of course with due apologies to Professor Heisenberg.

The question arises why do we need to do this?

Governments take decisions that are never recorded in writing. Even if they are, they are rarely revealed, not even after the prohibitory periods are over. For instance, the British system, despite being relatively open, is clouded in secrecy. Secret verbal decisions have invariably devolved on the man on the spot to execute. Such individuals have always enjoyed tremendous discretion in achieving the goals of the state.

One such British official was Lord Mountbatten. He enjoyed the confidence of both the King of England and the Prime Minister of the UK. Mountbatten was extremely discreet and never recorded in writing views or actions that conflicted with the British government's principled public position based on the British concept of fair play. Further, the kind of influence that Mountbatten and other British officials like General Lord Hastings Ismay, General Robert Lockhart, General Sir Francis

Roy Bucher, General Douglas Gracey and Field Marshal Claude Auchinleck exerted on decisions reflects patterns that a person with a discerning eye must reveal.

These patterns question the conventional explanation of the Partition of India and the consequent division of Jammu and Kashmir along the LoC and the Line of Actual Control (LAC).

I am not a historian; I studied science in school and economics in university. However, I was trained to develop an analytical ability and that has stood me in good stead while wearing the hat of a forensic investigator inquiring into the entire canvas of events surrounding the Partition of India in 1947.

My conclusion is that the Partition of India and the creation of the two Dominions of India and Pakistan were not the results of the freedom movement alone. Partition happened because the British could no longer trust the Indian Army's loyalty to the British Crown.

Here is the paradox. While the British had no choice but to dismantle the British Raj in India because of the aforementioned reason, they also had to stay on in the subcontinent for a very important reason—the British, despite being the closest US ally, were denied access to the results and secrets of the US nuclear programme. To build a credible nuclear deterrent against a probable Soviet bomb, they had to paradoxically spy on the Soviet nuclear programme from top-secret bases in Kashmir, Punjab and the North-West Frontier Province (NWFP). They had to, therefore, 'stay on' in the subcontinent till they had achieved the goal.

The British partially left India on 15 August 1947. However, India only emerged from the shadow of the Crown on 26 January 1950 when it became a republic.

It is not a well-publicised fact that Queen Elizabeth II was also the 'Queen of Pakistan' till 1956 when Pakistan was 'permitted' to become an Islamic republic and the British closed down their last base in Pakistan at Mauripur in Karachi. That was when they finally departed from the subcontinent, leaving behind in its wake a bitter trail of hatred and violence that endures till today.

Readers who wade through this book will find testable predictions that validate and support the aforementioned hypothesis. These predictions form part of the alternative pattern that tries to explain why Kashmir was divided into three parts between India, Pakistan and China. They reveal the intense British military presence in Pakistan, and why and how the British used their Pakistani proxies to invade Kashmir. It also reveals the fervent Soviet interest in both Kashmir and Aksai Chin. While the Soviets could not meet their objectives in the Valley and the Gilgit Agency, they were able to first fly the Chinese into Sinkiang and then get them to 'walk' into Aksai Chin. Thereafter, the Soviets were able to single-handedly extract uranium and other key minerals from Aksai Chin and ship them directly by road to the Soviet Union till the end of 1954. The famous road linking Sinkiang with western Tibet through Aksai Chin was initially only for use by Sino-Soviet Non-Ferrous and Rare Metals Company to transport freshly mined uranium ores to Khojand in what was then Soviet Tajikistan.

Because of regular overflights from Chaklala and Risalpur in Pakistan to the Soviet Union and Sinkiang, the British probably received warnings of Chinese activity in Sinkiang and Aksai Chin. They did not share this with India for a variety of reasons that are beyond the scope of this book. Readers may want to read my book *Red Fear: The China Threat* for more on this subject.

Suffice to say that I have tried to open the doorway into a whole new area of research for scholars and historians to grapple with in the years to come. My main desire is to question the contemporary history of India from 1947 to the 75th year of India's independence.

IMAGE I.1: Sketch map of Maharaja Hari Singh's kingdom of Jammu and Kashmir. Source: AIM Television Archives

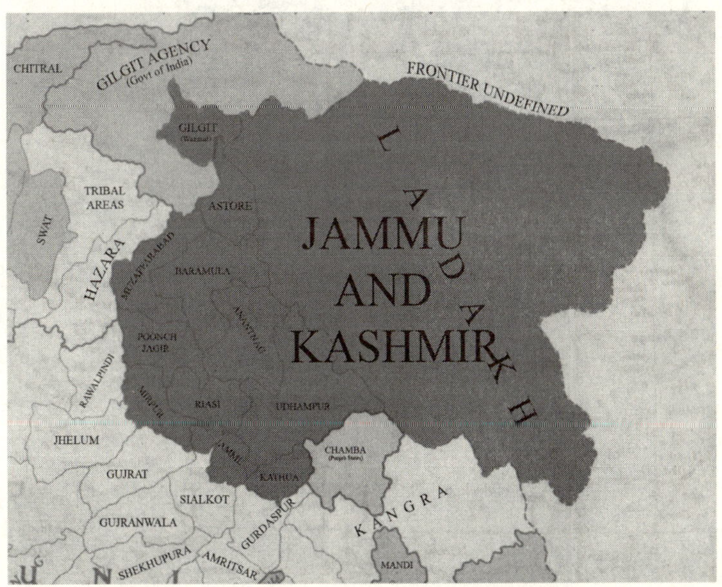

IMAGE I.2: Indicative map of north-west frontier of British India.
Source: AIM Television Archives

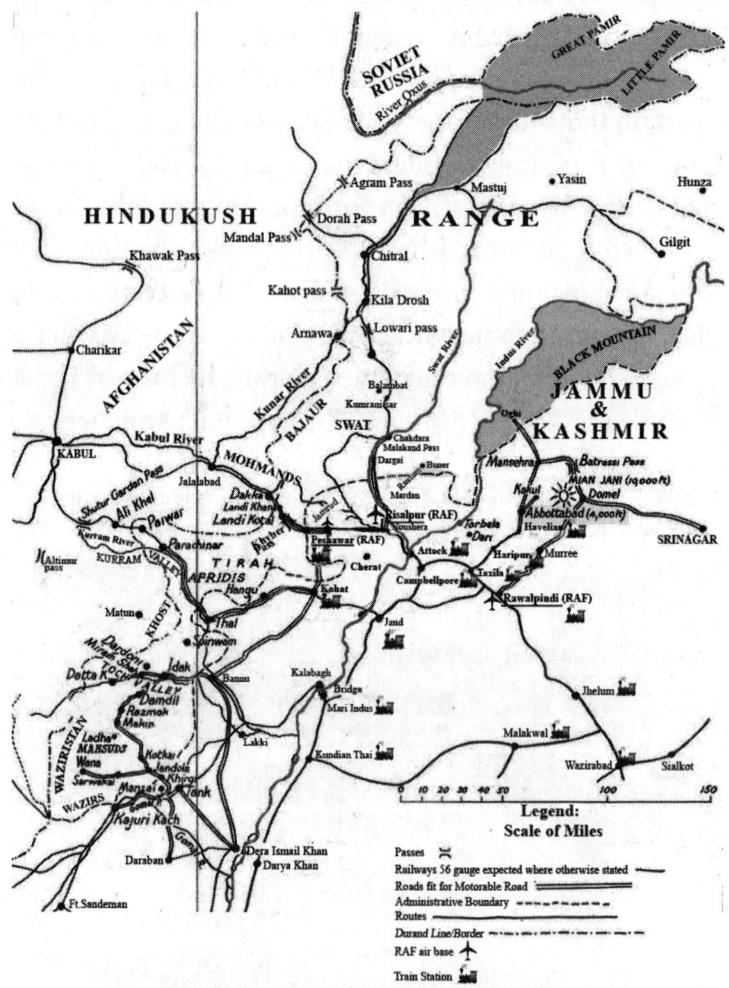

IMAGE I.3: Flying distance from Rawalpindi to Khojand (Leninabad).
Source: AIM Television Archives

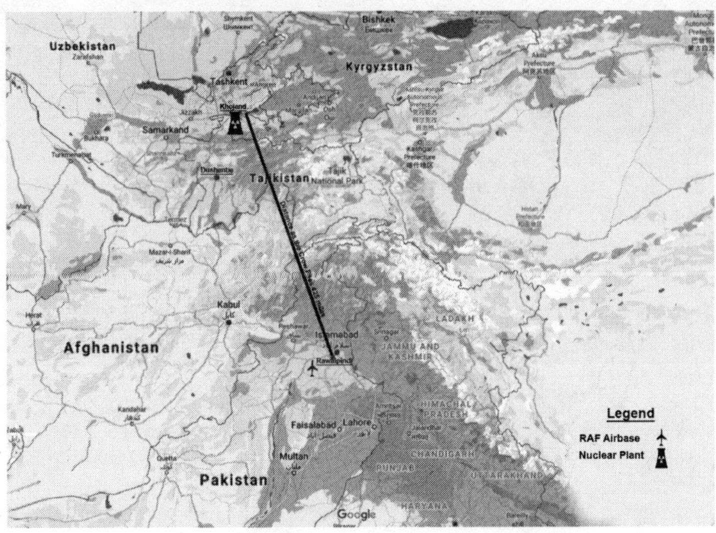

IMAGE I.4: Flying distance from Rawalpindi to Semey (Semipalatinsk).
Source: AIM Television Archives

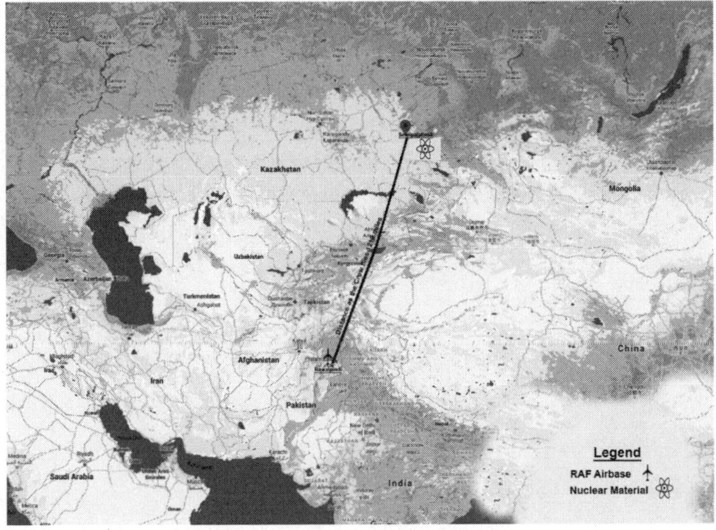

IMAGE I.5: Road and rail network for transhipment of uranium ore from Aksai Chin to Khojand (Leninabad). Source: AIM Television Archives

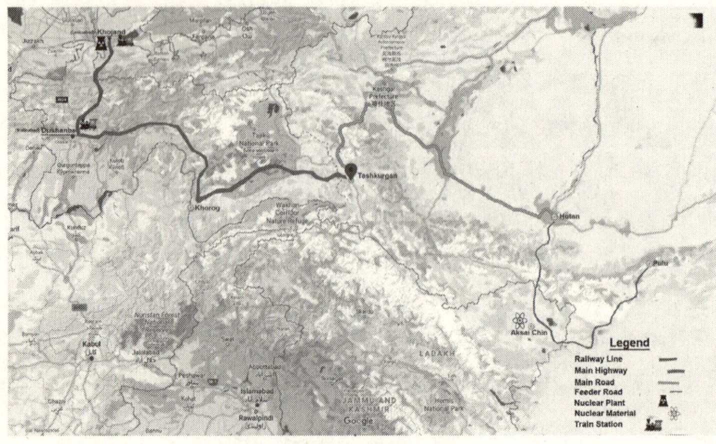

Chapter 1

Danger from the Pamirs

A British crisis and a Russian opportunity

In the first week of June 1891 in Tashkent, Colonel Mikhail Ionov walked into the luxurious office of the Russian Governor-General of Turkestan, Alexander Borisovich Vrevsky. Standing on the thick pile of a rust-coloured Bukhara carpet, Ionov smartly saluted Vrevsky. The latter was clearly worried over dispatches received from Nikolay Fyodorovich Petrovsky, Imperial Russian Consul General in Kashgar, Chinese Turkestan, some 600 kilometres away. These dispatches concerned the activities of Captain Francis Younghusband, an Indian Army officer who was transferred to the Indian Political Service (IPS). He was somewhat amateurishly plotting against the Russians in Kashgar.

IMAGE 1.1: Sir Francis Younghusband, 1905. Source: Wikipedia

Captain Younghusband had been sent to Kashgar exactly a year earlier in June 1890 to persuade the Chinese authorities to militarily secure their claim to the Pamir range of mountains. The need to do this had arisen because of what Younghusband had discovered the summer before he arrived in Kashgar. That summer, in 1889, Younghusband was dispatched to reconnoitre the region north of the Karakoram Pass. This was the area between the northern Karakoram and the southern Kunlun ranges. From Ladakh, Younghusband followed the Karakash River, which abruptly bends north-east near a place called Shahidullah, where the former Maharaja of Jammu and Kashmir Ranbir Singh had built a fort. However, towards the end of his reign, Maharaja Ranbir Singh was forced to abandon the fort because the Government of India was not in favour of Jammu and Kashmir making territorial inroads into Chinese Turkestan and following a foreign policy at variance with that of the Government of India's. The Government of India was wooing the somnambulant Qing Empire of China to become assertive and occupy unclaimed lands north of the Karakoram Mountain range so that they would become a buffer between the

IMAGE 1.2: Maharaja Ranbir Singh of Jammu and Kashmir.
Source: Wikipedia

British Raj and the then ever-expanding Russian Empire.

It was during this survey mission, sometime in October 1889, that Younghusband and his Gurkha escort entered the Shaksgam Valley from the north-east and stumbled upon a small detachment of Russian Cossack troops led by Major Bronislav Grombchevsky. One thing led to another and Grombchevsky invited Younghusband to dinner at his camp in the Raskam village on 23 October 1889. Younghusband was both intrigued and apprehensive about this invitation. Grombchevsky was the reason why the Foreign Secretary of India Sir Mortimer Durand sent Younghusband on this mission.

IMAGE 1.3: Captain Bronislav Grombchevsky of the Imperial Russian Army. Source: Wikipedia

In fact, a year earlier, in 1888, Grombchevsky arrived with his Cossack escort in Baltit, the capital of Hunza. The ruler of Hunza Mir Safdar Ali welcomed the Grombchevsky mission and eagerly concluded a tentative agreement on both the stationing of a permanent Russian post in Baltit and the training of the Hunza forces by the Russians.

Grombchevsky and his Cossack troops received Younghusband and his Gurkha detachment at the former's camp in Raskam. Vodka and brandy flowed freely when the two met. The gregarious Grombchevsky couldn't keep his mouth shut and by being loquacious and boastful, he created a chain reaction of events that has reverberated well into the 21st century. When Grombchevsky encountered Younghusband, he waved a Russian map in which the Wakhan region of Gilgit and the passes leading into Hunza were marked in red as areas belonging to Russia. The existence of this map, Grombchevsky's boastful proclamation that he was planning to travel further to Ladakh and the military mission that he was going to establish in Baltit perturbed Younghusband. He concluded that the Russians had plans to, at a minimum, take Gilgit. On his return to India, Younghusband filed his report with his superiors.

The Hunza Valley was strategically important to both the British Raj and Imperial Russia. Southwards, it opened to Gilgit, a key hub to India, Afghanistan and the warm waters of the Arabian Sea. Northwards, it opened to Imperial Russia, Imperial China and Central Asia. Hunza was the bridge at the crossroads of three

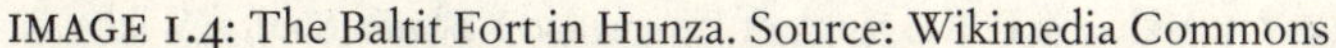

IMAGE 1.4: The Baltit Fort in Hunza. Source: Wikimedia Commons

empires vying for domination in Central Asia in the declining years of the 19th century.

Because Mir Safdar Ali and his immediate predecessor, Mir Ghazan Khan I, had been paying tribute to Jammu and Kashmir since 1870, Safdar Ali surreptitiously informed Pratap Singh, the eldest son of Maharaja Ranbir Singh, of these developments. In fact, Mir Ghazan Khan was the most loyal vassal of the Kashmir state and ever willing to send out recce survey parties to Chinese Turkestan to ascertain what parts of it could be safely nibbled away and added to the territories of Jammu and Kashmir.

Even though Pratap Singh was next in line to succeed his father, Maharaja Ranbir Singh, to the throne, Ranbir Singh wrote to the Government of India that he favoured his younger son Raja Amar Singh as his successor. However, the British struck

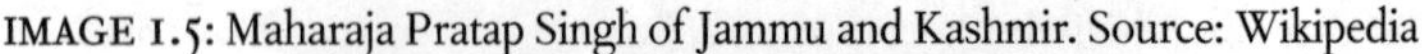
IMAGE 1.5: Maharaja Pratap Singh of Jammu and Kashmir. Source: Wikipedia

a deal with Pratap Singh and recognised him as the successor of Maharaja Ranbir Singh in return for permission for the Government of India to station a British Resident in Kashmir. In return, the Government of India recognised Pratap Singh as Maharaja, as opposed to his younger brother Raja Amar Singh as desired by their father, Maharaja Ranbir Singh. This was in 1885.

Despite the deal, Pratap Singh had an independent streak in him, and he concealed from the British the details of the correspondence between him and Mir Safdar Ali. However, someone in his court betrayed him. One of his brothers (or both) was probably responsible for this betrayal. The details of Pratap Singh's correspondence with Safdar Ali were revealed to the British Resident in Kashmir, Colonel Robert Parry Nisbet. Nisbet viewed this correspondence as an act of treason against the Government of India and in turn alerted the Viceroy, the Marquis of Lansdowne. The Viceroy instructed Nisbet to in-principle strip Pratap Singh of his sovereign authority for carrying out treasonable correspondence with the enemies of the British Empire. The state came under the rule of the Resident. For the public record, Pratap Singh voluntarily resigned his sovereignty in favour of the Council of Regency led by his two brothers, Ram Singh and Amar Singh, along with few key officials of the British-led Government of India. The Council of Regency, thereafter, reported directly to the British Resident on all important matters of foreign relations, with a warning that if the arrangement proved unsatisfactory in practise, the Government of India reserved the right to bring the region of Gilgit under its direct administrative control. This was in February 1889.

As a result of the events in Kashmir in the late 19th century, the Grombchevsky mission to Hunza had far-reaching consequences. The Government of India imposed direct rule in Jammu and Kashmir, dispossessing the Maharaja of the state. The Government of India then initiated the so-called Forward Policy for the first time and started sending out recce missions into Central Asia to ascertain real dangers caused by the Russian Empire to the British Raj in India.

The Gilgit Agency and the Wazarat of Gilgit

What was the state of affairs in neighbouring Gilgit?

In 1889, some four years after the creation of the office of the Resident in Kashmir, the Government of India created the Gilgit Agency and placed experienced field soldier Colonel Algernon Durand in command. It also appointed British officers to lead a combined force of Punjabi, Kashmiri and Gurkha fighting troops. Thereafter, Spedding, Dinga Singh and Company began the construction of the Gilgit Transport Road, a technological feat of 240-mile-long road from Srinagar to Gilgit town that combined tactical considerations with European engineering principles and materials.

IMAGE 1.6: Colonel Algernon Durand. Source: Public Domain

Both Government of India's Gilgit Agency and Kashmir's Wazarat were headquartered in Gilgit town, but they were separate enterprises, not a diarchy (joint rule). Two considerations were critical. First, the chain of command was as follows: the Governor of the Wazarat, the Wazir-i-Wazarat, reported to the Maharaja of Kashmir; the Gilgit Agency's Political Agent reported to the Government of India's Resident in Kashmir; and the Maharaja of Kashmir also reported to the Government of India's Resident, who in turn reported to the Viceroy of India. The Maharaja was never treated on a par with either the Resident or the Viceroy. Second, the Wazarat, which was less than a quarter of the size of the Gilgit Agency, must not be confused with the Gilgit district, which only took shape after the first Indo-Pakistani War of 1947–1948. The Wazarat included Gilgit tehsil, which encompassed Gilgit town and some outlying villages as well as Astor and Bunji.

Strictly speaking, the Gilgit Agency included the Gilgit Wazarat, but the Wazarat did not include the Gilgit Agency. The only portion of the Gilgit Agency that was under the direct control of the Kashmir Durbar was the Gilgit Wazarat comprising the tehsils of Gilgit and Astor and the Niabat of Bunji. Otherwise, the Political Agent in Gilgit was responsible to the Resident of Kashmir in Srinagar for the proper administration of the remaining districts commonly known as the political districts of the Gilgit Agency.

Throughout the first few months of 1890, the Government of India was busy strategising how to forestall the Russian threat. It all seemed too real. The

Viceroy of India Lord Lansdowne was not in favour of sharing a border with the Russians. He felt that it was better to create a neutral buffer between the British Raj and Imperial Russia. To this end, this buffer needed to be provided by the Afghans in the west and the Chinese in the east.

Younghusband is outsmarted by Petrovsky

As narrated earlier, to put this strategy in place, Lord Lansdowne sent Younghusband to Kashgar in June 1890 along with George McCartney, who was a half-Chinese half-British civil servant. McCartney spoke fluent Mandarin and his job was to convince the Qing authorities in Kashgar to assert their claims to the Pamirs as early as possible using soldiers on the ground. Younghusband's main interaction was with the District Commissioner, or Taotai, of Kashgar, and he used George McCartney as the translator in this exercise. However, Younghusband's candour did not earn him any brownie points with the Taotai, who was a master in the art of both statecraft and personal aggrandisement. While relaying the import of Younghusband's entreaties to his superiors and convincing them of the advantages involved in following Younghusband's suggestions, the Taotai had simultaneously sold himself to the Machiavellian Petrovsky and was duly reporting to the latter the contents of each of his interactions with both Younghusband and McCartney as often as they occurred, and also the instructions he received from his superiors. In this manner, the Russians, with their advance information of British intent and moves, were able to pre-empt the British plan. The Taotai disclosed to Petrovsky the fact that the Afghan troops were advancing to their side of the Pamirs, and that the Qing forces were being mobilised to do so. All this while, Younghusband was blissfully unaware of the scale of Taotai's betrayal.

Mikhail Ionov places Russia in control of the Pamirs

It was in this context that Vrevsky summoned Ionov to his office. Vrevsky ordered Ionov to immediately occupy the heights of the four Pamirs that ostensibly were near the Chinese side, namely the Kara Kol, Sarikol, Taghdumbash and Mariang, and the two Pamirs in Tajikistan that were near the Afghan side. This effectively meant that Russian forces were to take physical control of those 6 out of 11 Pamirs that the British were instigating the Afghans and Chinese to occupy. Further, on the north bank of the Oxus, Afghan Tajiks had crossed over and occupied the valleys. They were to be evicted and pushed south of the Oxus or Amu Darya. Additionally, Ionov was to displace any Chinese or Afghan garrisons that were to prove an impediment to the Russian consolidation of these territorial objectives.

IMAGE 1.7: A trooper from Colonel Ionov's Cossack Cavalry. Source: Wikipedia

The Russian troops under the command of the intrepid Ionov was a battalion-strong force of Cossacks. They encountered the Chinese Commander Chang's force at a site called Soma Tash, which meant 'written stone'. This site had a Chinese stone boundary marker that was believed to have been established in 1759 by Chinese Commander Fu Tajin, the leader of the Chinese Emperor Qianlong's expeditionary force sent to secure East Turkestan so that it could no longer serve as a doorway into Mongolia for Islamic invaders. Emperor Qianlong had no further territorial objectives. He wanted to warn his western neighbours to desist from all plans to attack Chinese interests. But in 1891, using this boundary marker, Commander Chang attempted to also claim the area between Alichur Pamir and Lake Yashil Kul in the Pamirs.

Ionov's response was to uproot the boundary marker, thereby erasing China's claim to the Alichur Pamir area.

Ionov's superior force overawed the Chinese contingent and the latter, bowing to superior strength, sensibly withdrew from the area. The boundary marker later landed up in a museum in Dushanbe, the capital of Tajikistan. Thereafter, the Russians travelled south towards the Hindu Kush Mountain range. The Hindu Kush is an 800-kilometre-long mountain range that stretches through Afghanistan to Chitral in Pakistan and into Tajikistan. It is the western flank of the Pamirs, the Karakoram and the Himalayas. It separates the valley of the Oxus River to the north from the Indus River valley to the south. To the north, near its north-eastern end, the Hindu Kush buttresses the Pamirs near the point where today the borders of China, Pakistan and Afghanistan meet, after which it runs south-west through Pakistan and into Afghanistan near their border.

The Russian force first traversed the Pamir River that formed the northern boundary of the Wakhan region. They then crossed the Wakhan River near Bozai Gumbaz, some 40 kilometres from the Vakhjir Pass, which is the only navigable pass that links the Wakhan region with Xinjiang. Finally, Ionov and his men crossed through the Darkot Pass, which connects the Barghol Valley in Chitral with the Rawat Valley in Ghizr district of Gilgit. From the Darkot Pass, Gilgit is only 134 kilometres and Baltit, the capital of Hunza, 121 kilometres.

When Ionov entered what was then the Gilgit Agency under the writ of the Resident Political Agent of the Government of India's Gilgit Agency, he transgressed into British territory. Ionov's transgression exposed the vulnerability of British rule and shredded the myth of the invincibility of the British Empire. The Hindu Kush was no longer a natural and secure barrier that could shield India against a Russian thrust.

Younghusband encounters Ionov

After surveying the routes from the Darkot Pass to Gilgit and Baltit, Ionov returned to the Pamirs on his way back. On the eventful date of 13 August 1891, Ionov met Younghusband near Bozai Gumbaz. Ionov was some 250 kilometres due south of the then official Russian border. During his foray into British India, he had probably travelled another 100 to 150 kilometres from the Russian border. It is safe to argue that Ionov penetrated non-Russian territories to a depth of 400 kilometres. This was unprecedented by all accounts. In this foray, Ionov not only overawed and routed the Chinese but also triumphantly entered British India and remained there at will, unmolested and unchallenged.

IMAGE 1.8: Indian Army Field Artillery led by elephants in the Pamirs in the 1880s. Source: Wikipedia

Ionov showed Younghusband a map that displayed the Russian border. The map not only included the six Pamirs but also extended to the Khora Bhurt Pass. This pass is 118 kilometres from Gilgit. It connects the upper Gilgit Valley in Ishkoman with the Wakhan Corridor. The Russian Bear was now breathing down the British Lion's mane. Ionov accused Younghusband of transgressing into Russian territory without proper paperwork and asked him to leave the Pamirs immediately. Ionov poured salt onto Younghusband's wounds after arresting him along with his travel companion and compatriot Lieutenant Davison near Bozai Gumbaz. This expulsion of two British officers, from what was believed to be Afghan territory, based on Russian maps, by a Russian military force that patrolled within a few days' marching distances to both Gilgit and Baltit, sent shudders down the spines of the Government of India and its British masters in London. Both the Baroghil and the Khora Bhurt passes also lead to Chitral in what was then the NWFP.

Thus, the Government of India discovered that—Ionov having surveyed all the routes to the Gilgit Agency, Hunza and Chitral from three different pivots, which themselves were far from their own perception of the Russian border—they could now no longer remain mute spectators to these developments. These entry points from the Hindu Kush into the British sphere of influence had to be blocked off.

Coinciding with the seasonal Russian withdrawal from the Pamirs just before the onset of winter, which made travelling difficult, the Government of India executed some deft moves. On 29 November 1891, Algernon Durand sent letters to the rulers of Hunza and Nagar, identifying them as 'feudatories' of the Government of India and claiming the government's obligatory right to enter and build a road through these territories to safeguard the Empire against Russian advances. He gave them a three-day ultimatum, after which government troops would enter their territories and start constructing a road regardless of any opposition they may offer. There could be no question of refusal. Fighting ensued, which lasted from 2 to 21 December 1891, and as British-led troops approached Nagar and Hunza, their leaders fled. The road encountered steep gradients, traversed canyons, ran through a snow-ravaged pass and established a supply line of rest stations. The road snaked through the 13,000-feet-high Mintaka Pass through the Karakoram to Kashgar in Sinkiang. The Government of India informed the opium-ravaged, weak and tottering Qing Court that Hunza, lying entirely to the south of the Hindu Kush, was within their sphere of influence.

Soon after the annexation of Hunza and Nagar, Chitral also came under the yoke of the Government of India. The vacuum created in the Pamirs by the seasonal withdrawal of Ionov and his Cossacks were filled by the Chinese in February 1892. The Chinese control was, however, short-lived, and in April 1892, a small force of Afghan troops seized Soma Tash. To save face, the Chinese declared that the area was indefensible and proposed for it to be declared a neutral zone.

The Chinese lost face elsewhere as well. In 1892, British and Chinese officers jointly approved the installation of a new Hunza ruler, Mir Muhammad Nazim Khan, and on 15 September of the same year, two Chinese officers attended his formal installation where Sanad XVI (agreement), drafted and choreographed by the British, was formalised at Baltit Fort. On that occasion, as instructed by the British, the Nawab, Mir Nazim, informed the Chinese officers he could no longer accept gifts (tribute exchange) from China. This formalised the sequestration of Hunza from the Chinese sphere of influence in the presence of Chinese officers.

After annexing Hunza in 1892, the Government of India partially restored power to Maharaja Pratap Singh on the condition that '[he] shall give [his] utmost assistance to promote the affairs of Gilgit in accordance with the instructions of the Government of India'. The Maharaja was shown his place—he was a vassal to a superior power. The hegemon continued to treat the Maharaja with contempt.

Ionov returns and his impact propels a settlement

The Afghan border troops stayed at Soma Tash for a brief period before being ordered to leave once Ionov returned after the snow melted. Their doughty commander tried to resist but was hopelessly outnumbered. Fifteen out of seventeen Afghans were killed. Russia now became the dominant force in this area by virtue of its physical presence. In the spring of 1893, the Russians constructed the Pamirsky Post in the village of Murghab in today's Tajikistan. This was a fortress to house the Cossacks involved in patrolling the

Pamirs. Thereafter, Ionov established another military base near Khorog in the summer of 1894. The Russians were here to stay permanently.

These developments did not bode well for the Government of India. The Government of India and its British masters were chary of spending money to police this far-flung region. Yet it could not be ignored or neglected because of what Ionov had demonstrated. Ionov had exposed the cracks in the defence of British India. These cracks had to be papered over. Perhaps, it was time to rehabilitate the Chinese and once again drag them into the game as buffers?

IMAGE 1.9: British troops fighting with tribals in Chitral, 1895.
Source: Wikipedia

Meanwhile, the British were frantically seeking a solution to sanctify the frontier to ring-fence Ionov and prevent him from increasing the Russian remit in the Gilgit Agency. Their efforts paid off since Czar Nicholas II was quite the favourite grandson of Queen Victoria. Thus, on 11 March 1895, both Great Britain and Russia agreed to demarcate the Pamirs, though without the participation and consent of the Qing Empire. Between 22 July and 10 September 1895, the Anglo-Russian Boundary Commission defined the boundaries with key landmarks. Afghanistan was brought in as a buffer, and the only point of convergence between the British Raj, Imperial Russia and Qing China was at the easternmost point of the newly created Wakhan Corridor near the peak of Kokrash Kol. The Government of India was the real gainer through this agreement, even though Russia was able to extend its remit to a large part of the Pamirs. However, the Russian advance towards the south under Ionov was halted from Sarakhs in the west on the present-day Iran-Turkmenistan border, to the Taghdumbash Pamir in the east in Hunza. This latter area was ceded to China by Pakistan in 1963. Further, the northern side of the Hindu Kush Mountain range was effectively demilitarised and the prevailing threat from Russia extinguished.

In 1894, the government once again permitted the Hunza-China tribute exchange to resume. They also searched for a cost-effective solution to the cracks opened up by the Pamir forays of the Russians. The return of the Chinese buffer was one such solution. This required the Government of India to pull out their troops and personnel from Hunza in 1896.

This did not in any way change the prohibition of the Maharaja's access to and rights over Hunza and Nagar. The opportunistic wedge separating suzerainty from sovereignty did not settle well with the Maharaja. He learned that Hunza and Nagar were 'Kashmir feudatories' 'under Kashmir suzerainty' and that they were 'not Kashmir territory'. Keeping Jammu and Kashmir out of Hunza and Nagar was sustained as indicated in a collected file of the Gilgit Agency matters of over three decades. Letter No. 1800-F, dated 24 July 1901, addressed to the British Resident Sir A. Talbot, laid the following foundation in which the tracts, namely Chilas, Khizr Kuh, Yasin and Yashkoman, though under the suzerainty of Jammu and Kashmir, were not Jammu and Kashmir territory and Kashmir officials were not allowed to interfere in their internal administration. The territory was well nuanced. India was Gilgit Agency. Jammu and Kashmir was Wazarat. Separately, the Gilgit Agency's writ was extended through a process of salami slicing, and it absorbed Chilas and Gor in 1893, Khizr Kuh in 1895, and Yasin and Yashkoman in 1895; it also oversaw the political districts of Chitral, Hunza and Nagar, which were under Jammu and Kashmir's suzerainty but were not Jammu and Kashmir's territory. They were part of the Government of India's territory.

Both Britain and Russia were seeking ways to preserve the peace and avoid conflicts. This was partly because of the familial links between their royal families and partly because they were unwilling to pay the financial costs of endless conflicts. Consequently, in 1903–1904, they started formal talks, which concluded with the Anglo-Russian Convention of 1907. In Asia, the game of brinkmanship between Britain and Russia that almost led to war had been averted.

British deviousness not only neutralised possible Russian forays into the region known as the Gilgit Agency, but it also kept the Maharaja out of the picture and blocked any possible future alliance between the Maharaja and the Russians. The Maharaja had caved in without any resistance. There was no diarchy at all. Britain continuously pursued administrative practices with such finesse that the Maharaja's rule over his Wazarat was impotent, to put it mildly.

At the dawn of the 20th century, the military administration over the Gilgit Agency gave way to an administrative rule that further made invisible the Maharaja's administration of his Wazarat. The Maharaja did not collect taxes or deploy troops outside his Wazarat or exercise any judicial control. The writ of the Ranbir Penal Code did not extend out there unlike in the Valley or Jammu. The Maharaja neither extended his writ in Hunza nor was the state flag ever raised there. Also, the ruler of Hunza never acknowledged the writ of the Maharaja. Further, the British officials established the Agency with its own departments of agriculture, public works, education and forestry. All Government of India's officials running the Agency lived in Gilgit town. The Agency raised its own local militia called Gilgit Scouts, which was directly under the control of British officers.

IMAGE 1.10: National Military Memorial, Bengaluru, to honour those who lost their lives in NWFP in 1915. Source: Wikimedia Commons

Archival records do not reveal the existence of any substantive or conclusive British documents on the Gilgit Agency because of the perceived British practice of not committing to writing sensitive matters that could be verbally decided. Furthermore, rarely were matters cross-referenced in writing, and all top-secret files on the Gilgit region were destroyed at Partition because of the continuing sensitivity of the Gilgit region to the British till the end of 1956.

Also, the Government of India's standard bureaucratic practices regularly transferred officers on short-term posts and produced layers within layers of secret divisions of ignorance about and in other divisions of its labyrinthine bureaucracy. The conclusions arrived at here have been reached through an exhaustive process of joining the dots in hindsight. This approach reveals that the British-run Government of India's Gilgit Agency and presumed territory belonged to Maharaja Hari Singh's kingdom of Jammu and Kashmir only for a brief period of few months beginning from 31 July 1947, when the Gilgit lease was rescinded, till 31 October 1947, when control of the Gilgit Agency reverted to the British. As we shall see in later pages of this book, the Gilgit lease was revoked by Lord Mountbatten because he was supremely confident that Maharaja Hari Singh's kingdom was going to accede to Pakistan. Because that did not happen, it became imperative to engineer the Gilgit rebellion to sequester the Agency from the kingdom and give the region to Pakistan. In later pages, my argument identifies China as the undisclosed protagonist in a puzzle that first began with the Russian thrust into Hunza.

Chapter 2

Soviet Control of Sinkiang Influences British Policy in Kashmir

A ring-fenced Maharaja

The restoration of the Maharaja's rule in 1905 was not a reversal to the status quo ante that existed in 1889 when he was dispossessed. Riders were imposed on the Maharaja's authority and he was effectively ring-fenced by the Government of India.

The Maharaja could not take any consequential decision without the consent of the Government of India's plenipotentiary, the Resident. Furthermore, the British policy of divide and rule was used to the hilt by the Resident, who encouraged Amar Singh to shadow every action of the Maharaja. For his loyalty to the Government of India, Amar Singh was rewarded with the guarantee that his only son, Hari Singh, born in 1895, would succeed Pratap Singh as the next Maharaja. This was in line with the principle of primogeniture, given that Hari Singh was a direct male descendant of Maharaja Gulab Singh. Further, given the distrust between Pratap Singh and the Government of India, the latter was never going to endorse any of Pratap Singh's nominees.

The combined issue of dispossession, restoration and succession overwhelmed Pratap Singh throughout his constrained reign, but the issue of succession was the most important of the lot. Besides Amar Singh, Pratap Singh had another younger brother named Raja Ram Singh, who died childless. Relations between Pratap Singh and Amar Singh, which had been contentious even when Maharaja Ranbir Singh was alive, became worse during the period when the British Resident directly ruled the state, a period that also saw Amar Singh's political ambitions peak. The question of deciding Pratap Singh's successor gained more traction from 1889 onwards. He was childless after he lost his only son in infancy. Visibly shattered after a 16-year-long limbo in his rule, Pratap Singh decided to retaliate after he was reinstated as the ruler of the state in 1905. In 1906, it was rumoured that Pratap Singh intended to adopt a distant male relative ostensibly for religious purposes. The larger plan was to exclude Hari Singh from the succession. The Government of India took up the case with the Maharaja and pointed out that he should not adopt a distant relative, especially when he had a brother and a nephew. Refusing to comply, Pratap Singh pointed out the impracticality of the option being given Amar Singh was too old to adopt a son, and Hari Singh could not be adopted under the Hindu law because he was Amar Singh's only son. When J.D. Mayne's *Treatise on Hindu Law and Usage* was consulted, his argument was annulled. Yet, he insisted on adopting a distant relation, citing religious requirements. He argued that in Hinduism when one did not have a son, he had to adopt one so that the adopted son could perform the annual *shraddha* or ritual remembrance of his departed father. The Viceroy of India then clearly informed Pratap Singh of the Government of India's decision to appoint Amar Singh and his son, Hari Singh, as Pratap Singh's successor.

The embittered Pratap Singh never accepted this decision, and despite the Viceroy's communication on the subject, in 1907, he adopted Jagat Dev Singh of Poonch, a descendant of Raja Dhyan Singh, the younger brother of Maharaja Gulab Singh. The Government of India then wrote to him informing him that this adoption would not affect the rights of Pratap Singh's closest relatives.

The emergence of Anglo-Soviet antagonism

While the Anglo-Russian Convention of 1907 secured the British enough to reinstate the Maharaja, the Government of India could not let its guard down for too long. The Russian Revolution of 1917 and the British support of the White Armies re-established the rivalry between Britain and Russia. The embattled Bolshevik regime in Russia, which was fighting the pro-Western White Armies during the Russian Civil War, decided to establish the Comintern (Communist International), or the Third International, in March 1919. The leaders of Bolshevik Russia announced that the only way they could preserve the revolution was to fight back against Western powers and spread communism throughout the world via the Comintern.

IMAGE 2.1: Major General Wilfrid Malleson of the Indian Army.
Source: Wikipedia

The obvious corollary of this decision was to take the fight to India, the jewel in the crown of the British Empire. Earlier in July 1918, Major General Sir Wilfrid Malleson of the Indian Army led an expedition of both British and Indian troops to Turkestan, Russia, during the Civil War. The Indian troops of the 19th

Punjab Rifles engaged Bolshevik forces and defeated them in Merv, in what is present-day Turkmenistan. This was the first direct military confrontation between British and Russian troops since the Crimean War of 1853–1854. The 19th Punjab Rifles contingent was reinforced in September 1918 by troops of the 28th Light Cavalry, which was merged into the 7th Light Cavalry in post-independent India. The Indian troops fought in Kaka, Arman Sagad and Dushak, but because of the collapse of anti-Bolshevik forces in April 1919, Malleson was forced to withdraw from Russian Turkestan the same month. The reach of the British Empire was finally being extended up to Russia.

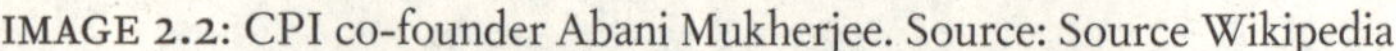
IMAGE 2.2: CPI co-founder Abani Mukherjee. Source: Source Wikipedia

Wary of the British might, the Bolsheviks decided to counter-attack with a political gambit. The Comintern, therefore, organised the First Congress of the Peoples of the East in Baku in September 1920. The congress specifically aimed at fighting imperialism in Asia. Baku, in Soviet-controlled Azerbaijan, was only 2,000 kilometres from Merv. Tashkent, where the Communist Party of India (CPI) was formed on 17 October 1920, was only 900 kilometres away from Merv. The CPI's two main founders of Indian origin were M.N. Roy and Abani Mukherjee.

IMAGE 2.3: CPI co-founder M.N. Roy. Source: Wikipedia

The seeds of the old British-Russian enmity now flowered into a new confrontation between the Government of India and Soviet Russia. Kashmir once again became the underbelly of this dispute. Abani Mukherjee, an associate of Rash Behari Bose, was jailed in Singapore for procuring weapons for use in the Hindu-German conspiracy of 1914–1917. The objective of this conspiracy was to foment rebellion in the Indian Army. Mukherjee escaped from the Fort Canning prison in Singapore in 1917 and made his way to Moscow. M.N. Roy, who also participated in the Hindu-German conspiracy, escaped from British detention and made his way to Moscow via the US and Mexico.

The Government of India restrengthens its hold on Kashmir

It was against this backdrop in 1920 that a worried Government of India established the Council of State in Kashmir. This was a successor to the Council of Regency, which was dissolved in 1905. In many ways, the clock had once again been turned back. After Amar Singh died in 1910, his son and British-supported heir to the throne of Jammu and Kashmir, Hari Singh, took his father's place as a senior member of the council. His task was to shadow the Maharaja in much the same way his father had done in the past. This further fuelled Pratap Singh's animosity towards Hari Singh, who was foisted upon him by the British. Pratap Singh died a frustrated, embittered man in 1925 after spending 36 of the 40 years of his rule being ring-fenced and downsized, far removed from the glory of his grandfather, Maharaja Gulab Singh.

The wheel of time had turned full circle. The Government of India was not confident enough about the loyalty of Pratap Singh and considered him a weak link in the overall strategic challenge that Jammu and Kashmir faced. The government had no choice but to intervene in the state's functioning. Autonomy for the ruler or even the empowerment of an at-arm's-length relative was not an option. This policy towards the state government continues to be followed today in 21st-century India. Rulers, politicians and civil servants have come and gone, but the Government of India is still the overarching central authority that firmly continues to exercise its control over Jammu and Kashmir. The challenges that the state faces have remained the same, and the options to deal with them have also remained pretty much the same as they were in the 19th century.

On 23 September 1925, Maharaja Pratap Singh passed away. Although Hari Singh was in line to succeed the late King, two issues muddied the situation even as the Maharaja's last rites were yet to be performed. The state was governed by the Council of State since 1920, so the Resident, Sir John Wood, was to officially recognise Hari Singh as the new Maharaja. But Wood was away on tour in Hunza, so his first assistant, knowing Raja Jagat Dev Singh's claim to the throne, decided to directly communicate to Hari Singh that the Government of India recognised him as the new Maharaja. Despite this act of apparent goodwill, far from experiencing a smooth succession, Hari Singh was shocked when the Viceroy's condolence telegram addressed him as Raja Hari Singh instead of Maharaja. This, he feared, put him in the same status as the late Maharaja's adopted son, Raja Jagat Dev Singh.

The problem did not end there. According to the rules of succession of a natural heir in the direct line, a prince succeeded his demised father as a matter of course, and the succession was recognised by an exchange of formal letters, or *kharita*s, between the new ruler and the Viceroy of India. The Viceroy had to first recognise and accept the succession of the new ruler, and only after that could the exchange of *kharitas* take place. Hari Singh's succession was peculiar because he was not the late Maharaja's son and was, therefore, not a natural heir in the direct line of succession. His succession had to be both recognised and confirmed by the Viceroy before there could be an exchange of *kharitas* between the two of them. And then there was a concern over the late Maharaja's adopted son, Raja Jagat Dev Singh, who was also a member of the Council of State.

The Government of India never trusted Pratap Singh and by extension also mistrusted Jagat Dev Singh. It was not willing to take a risk by giving the warring siblings the benefit of the doubt because, technically speaking, Jagat Dev Singh was also of the same bloodline, an equally direct descendant of Mian Kishore Singh, the common great-great-grandfather of Jagat Dev Singh and Hari Singh.

Hari Singh's claim to the throne rested on his father Amar Singh's unwavering loyalty to the Government of India, and Hari Singh's perception was that he was a much safer bet for British interests. Of course, future events were to prove otherwise.

Maharaja Hari Singh's defiant streak

Hari Singh first revealed his independent thoughts by objecting to the government's delay in confirming his succession. He believed that his succession had already been endorsed by both the Government of India and Maharaja Pratap Singh while he was still alive. He did not buy the government's defence of the distinction between a natural heir in the direct line and an heir presumptive and was dismissive of the process and procedures laid down in the law. The British, however, were sticklers for these details. After much deliberation and obtaining the Secretary of State's consent, the Viceroy finally presented the *kharita* of offerings to Hari Singh on 14 October 1925. For three long weeks, the issue of succession had remained unresolved. Hari Singh's bitterness towards the British and their tardiness began to colour his perception of them and their interests. The British were stuck on the horns of a dilemma. Their chosen domino displayed a streak of impatience and imperiousness. Could they continue to trust him? They weighed in on the option of Raja Jagat Dev Singh. Though he had supported his adoptive father in all proceedings of the Council of State and had remained an obedient and faithful son, could he have proven to be a more malleable domino?

In the end, the British cast their lot with Hari Singh but only after the Resident privately read out the riot act to Hari Singh and secured his consent to the long-established practice of non-interference in the frontier areas by state officials. He also agreed that state officials would take no action in Ladakh without consulting the British Joint Commission. But this episode ended the untrammelled hegemony of the British in the state as Hari Singh kept standing up against the British on several issues, gradually culminating in the events of August 1947 when he thwarted British designs and took decisions that ultimately led to the division of the state along military lines between India and Pakistan. His actions also resulted in the Congress-led Indian government deposing him from his throne, just as the British had done to his predecessor, Maharaja Pratap Singh.

Maharaja Hari Singh inherited a state that had an overwhelmingly large Muslim population. This was a unique political situation where a Hindu ruler was ruling over a Muslim majority. The situation in the rest of India, till the advent of British rule in 1757, had been the very opposite.

Hari Singh's new enemies emerge

After Hari Singh acceded to the throne, an organisation called Anjuman-e-Nusrat-ul-Islam, founded in 1905 by the Maulvi of Srinagar's Jamia Masjid, started a movement calling for the educational emancipation of Kashmiri Muslims. As a result, many Kashmiri Muslims went to study at universities all over India. In 1931, among the first Kashmiri graduates to return to Srinagar were Sheikh Mohammed Abdullah, Mirza Afzal Beg and G.M. Sadiq. These young men got politically involved and stood in opposition to the Maharaja's perceived autocracy. This opposition was triggered by a succession of incidents in Jammu wherein some state government officials purportedly demolished a mosque. When the news reached Srinagar, it caused public outrage. On 25 June 1931, a Pakhtoon man called Abdul Qadeer made a seditious speech against the Maharaja's rule. He was arrested and put on trial in Srinagar on 4 July 1931.

IMAGE 2.4: Sheikh Abdullah (third from left) with other leaders of the agitation of 1931. Source: Wikimedia Commons

On 13 July 1931, while Qadeer's trial was on in the Srinagar Central Jail, the police opened fire on an unruly mob of Qadeer supporters, killing 22 demonstrators. The agitation then spread throughout the state. The Maharaja was convinced that a senior minister in his court, a British bureaucrat named G.E.C. Wakefield, was the brain behind this agitation and immediately dismissed him. The Maharaja believed that the agitation

was a pre-planned attack on him, a punishment for taking a contradictory stance against the British at the Round Table Conference in London in 1930. Wakefield was replaced by a distinguished Kashmiri Pandit Sir Hari Kishan Kaul, who was made the state's Prime Minister.

The agitation throughout Kashmir was spearheaded by two men: a religious leader called Mirwaiz Mohammad Yusuf Shah and his protégé, a young schoolmaster called Sheikh Mohammed Abdullah. The agitation led by these two men with the support of other Muslim leaders in the country forced the Maharaja to set up a commission of enquiry that would investigate this violence. The commission presided over by Sir Bertram Glancy asked Hari Singh to create a constitution for the state that would enshrine freedom of speech, expression and assembly for its inhabitants. At the same time, Sheikh Abdullah and the Mirwaiz were imprisoned in Srinagar Central Jail. Their arrest added to their popularity, and they found a dedicated population of followers in the state. In 1934, the promised constitution was introduced in the state of Kashmir. This was the first time that the government imposed a constitution upon a princely state. The document guaranteed certain fundamental rights and forced Hari Singh to concentrate on his subjects and their political and economic needs.

Just as Pratap Singh's political freedoms were heavily constrained, Hari Singh's powers were also brought to check by the imposition of the constitution. The introduction of the constitution enabled some of the agitators to act upon and consolidate the power gained from the political mobilisation of 1931. Sheikh Abdullah and Mirwaiz Mohammad Yusuf Shah, while still in prison, orchestrated the establishment of a political party called the Muslim Conference in 1932, which brought together all political forces that opposed the Maharaja's rule. Though the princely state of Jammu and Kashmir now had a legal and lawful political Opposition, it was far from being a perfect democratic arrangement.

Hari Singh's Dogra community, the Valley's Sikh population who lived there since the time of Maharaja Ranjit Singh's conquest, and the Hindu Kashmiri Pandits all stood at the receiving end of the ever-growing strength of the Maharaja's Muslim subjects. The political mobilisation of the large Muslim population created a communal divide. Maharaja Hari Singh was outsmarted by the British, who very deftly engineered a deepening rift in the former's political power and authority.

However, rising differences between Sheikh Abdullah and Mohammad Yusuf Shah gave the Maharaja some breathing space. Sheikh Abdullah, then a 29-year-old, acquired a progressively cosmopolitan outlook while studying at Aligarh. He made peace with the Maharaja and upon his release from prison in 1933, married the half-Kashmiri daughter of Harry Nedou, the extremely wealthy Croatian proprietor of a chain of hotels in the state. Already enamoured by progressive political ideas, Abdullah's outlook on politics underwent further changes when he met Pandit Jawaharlal Nehru in 1938. Abdullah embraced the political lineage of the Congress party and began to operate the Muslim Conference as an extension of the Congress party in Jammu and Kashmir. His new and progressive ideas clashed with the ultra-conservative religious mindset of the Mirwaiz.

A split in the Muslim Conference was inevitable given the rising differences between the two leaders. Unable to work together, they finally dissolved the Muslim Conference in 1939. In its place, Abdullah founded the National Conference, a secular and progressive body where Islamic theology gave way to more pressing issues such as land reforms. In 1941, following the announcement of the Pakistan Resolution in Lahore, many Muslims in the state, disgruntled with Abdullah and the secular nature of the National Conference, convinced the Mirwaiz to resurrect the Muslim Conference. The newly resurrected organisation became the trump card for both Mohammed Ali Jinnah and the Muslim League. The National Conference, with its secular agenda, and the Muslim Conference, with its rabidly communal agenda, spearheaded the political struggles against the Maharaja's rule.

For a decade, the political opposition to the Maharaja's rule was legally mobilised under two different ideological strains. The British had succeeded in gradually eroding the omniscience of the Maharaja and had ensured the institutionalisation of a process that caused him continuous problems and ultimately unseated him. The 1934 constitution lasted only five years. A relentless protest campaign by the majority of Muslim politicians forced the Maharaja to scrap the constitution in favour of a new one in 1939. The crown of thorns that sat on the Maharaja's head since the 1930 Round Table Conference in London never gave him a moment of peace.

Soviets in Sinkiang knocking on Kashmir's northern doors

One of the reasons behind the introduction of the constitution in 1934 was to keep the Maharaja preoccupied with political changes in the Valley and to deflect his attention away from the state's northern borders. Maharaja Hari Singh's state of Jammu and Kashmir shared roughly 700-kilometre-long border with neighbouring Sinkiang. During this period, in neighbouring Sinkiang, Sheng Shicai, also known as Sheng-ts'ai, a Chinese warlord, took control over most of the region. Sheng Shicai was a Manchurian born Han Chinese who became Military Governor of Sinkiang on 12 April 1933. This development was dangerous for the Government of India because Sheng was in close contact with the Soviets who occupied Sinkiang in 1933–1934 to prevent any Japanese thrust into Siberia via the Gobi Desert. The Soviet fear arose because of an intrusion into Sinkiang between 1918 and 1921 by Japanese military officers. The Japanese established a powerful strategic and commercial spy ring. There was a high chance that Sinkiang would become a Soviet puppet state or be completely absorbed into the Soviet Union. The Main Intelligence Directorate of the Red Army (GRU) set up shop in Sinkiang in 1933–1934 and floated a local affiliate called the Bureau of Public

Safety, which spread its writ over the entire territory. Only nominal allegiance was shown to the Kuomintang Party of China (KMT)-controlled Republic of China. Sheng was to the Soviets in Sinkiang exactly what the deposed last Emperor of China Pu Yi was to the Japanese in Manchuria.

The almost permanent presence of the Red Army in Sinkiang alarmed the Government of India. In fact, in 1935, rumours spread in the Chinese capital of Nanking about the imminent Soviet invasion of the Kashmiri vassal state of Hunza. The Soviet sphere of influence was clearly marked along the entire Karakoram Mountain range. A string of forts was built along the border and manned by Soviet troops. The Red Army was at India's doors. Sinkiang's capital, Tihwa, was nicknamed 'Little Moscow'. Further, Sheng Shicai's rival Ma Hu-shan lived in Khotan, close to the Ladakh border. He planned an anti-Soviet jihad and the 'liberation' of the Soviet Union and India, both of which were to be brought under Islamic rule.

The natural barrier of the Karakoram Mountains could not keep agent provocateurs from infiltrating into British India and corrupting Indian politicians with the Bolshevik virus, a term used for Soviet or Comintern agents in the period during the First and Second World Wars. Sheng's main opponent, the Islamic warlord Ma Hu-shan, was then living in Khotan close to the Ladakh border, and there was a big chance that he would spread his control into northern Ladakh, where there were no Indian Army units stationed and the borders were not defined. Thus, in 1934, the entire state was potentially under threat.

IMAGE 2.5: (L–R) Sardar Vallabhbhai Patel, Bakshi Ghulam Mohammed and Sheikh Abdullah. Source: Wikipedia

In New Delhi, officials were extremely worried about the intent and actions of Hari Singh. Once again, as in Pratap Singh's time, the northern threat dominated the discourse. Ever since Hari Singh participated in the Round Table Conference in 1930, serious doubts were raised about his loyalty and cooperation in the event of an emergency, which greatly worried government officials. Moreover, the internal situation in Gilgit was confusing. While communication and defence in both the Agency and the Wazarat were handled by the

British, the civil government in the Wazarat was still controlled by the Maharaja through his Governor.

Interestingly, in 1931, when there were riots in Srinagar, the British tried to persuade the Maharaja to take on greater financial responsibility for the Corps of Gilgit Scouts, who were the primary defence forces in the region. This was because the Great Depression of the 1930s had affected the Indian government's budget. The Maharaja sat over this proposal until mid-1933 and presented a set of counter-proposals. He was ready to take on the entire financial burden for the defence of Gilgit provided the system of coexistence of the Agency and the minuscule Wazarat was terminated and complete sovereign authority returned to the Governor. Hari Singh's sights were clearly set on exploiting the situation in Sinkiang and using it to his advantage. The British, in the meanwhile, parried the Maharaja's growing political ambitions by acting upon the Glancy Commission proposal to introduce a constitution in the state, thereby leaving the Maharaja enmeshed in coping with internal dissent in the Valley. The Government of India got the opportunity it was looking for and sought to secure to itself all rights in the region.

Formal negotiations between the Maharaja and New Delhi began in October 1934 right after the constitution was introduced. The Maharaja was represented by his Prime Minister, Colonel Elliot James Dowell Colvin, and the Government of India was represented by the Resident in Kashmir, Lieutenant Colonel L.E. Lang, assisted by B.J. Glancy, who forced the constitutional change on the Maharaja. New Delhi did not alter its overwhelming advantage over the Maharaja of Kashmir. In 1934, Regulation No. 1 of Samwat 1991 established the Praja Sabha or State Legislative Assembly, which shall make the law for the whole state or any part thereof with two added restrictions. The Praja Sabha had no power over matters of security of British India and frontier policy, including those relating to Ladakh and Gilgit. Importantly, Ladakh, which included Baltistan and Gilgit's separate and independent status, was written into the Jammu and Kashmir state's constitution, which negated any prior or existing claim of British-Kashmir diarchy over the Gilgit Agency.

On 26 March 1935, the Maharaja leased the Gilgit Wazarat north of the Indus to the British for 60 years. The Gilgit Agency and the vassal states were already under the administration and control of the Government of India. The annual lease, a paltry sum of 1,250 rupees, was paid to the Maharaja in a lump sum of 75,000 rupees. On 1 October 1935, the British Political Agent in Gilgit, Major G. Kirkbride, took absolute charge of the region.

Thereafter in 1938, on Soviet instructions, Sheng closed the Khunjerab Pass, the trade route between Sinkiang and Gilgit, and the Karakoram Pass, the trade route between Sinkiang and Leh. This was because a number of local warlords from Sinkiang were using these passes to escape into the Gilgit region and Ladakh. The two most notable of these warlords were Mahmud and Ma Hu-shan. The British defence forces were now worried if military refugees could reach Leh via Aksai Chin, up the Karakash River from Khotan, would India not be under serious threat if more such warlords were able to enter Sinkiang?

The British were left in a diplomatic limbo. The KMT had no control but falsely claimed it. The Soviet Union had control but denied it. The frontier was closed. The Soviets had a monopoly over Sinkiang's trade and the exploitation of its mineral, tin, gold and oil wealth. All of this activity was routed through a Soviet organisation called Sovsintorg. The British rule in India depended upon the maintenance of Chinese integrity in Sinkiang as a neutral buffer between the British and the Soviets. The buffer vanished at the same time the penetration of a large number of communists into the Congress party began.

Chapter 3

Anglo-Soviet Rivalry Takes Political Shape Within India

The Soviet attempt to hijack the leadership of the Congress party

For the British, the greatest worry was the infiltration of communists, crypto-communists and sundry revolutionaries into the Congress party. A key communist agent provocateur to join the Congress party was M.N. Roy, who was himself the co-founder of the CPI in 1920. For the record, Roy defied the Comintern order to boycott the Congress party. Who knows whether or not this was merely a cover to admit ex-communists into the Congress party by showing that they had 'broken free' from the dictates of the Comintern? Roy urged Indian communists to join the Congress party to radicalise it. Nehru, in his presidential address at the Faizpur session of the Congress in December 1936, said this of Roy:

> [T]hough young, [he] is an old and well-tried soldier in India's fight for freedom. Comrade M.N. Roy has just come to us after a long and most distressing period in prison, but though shaken up in body, he comes with a fresh mind and heart, eager to take part in that old struggle that knows no end till it ends in success.

From the podium in Faizpur, Roy recommended the capturing of Congress Legislature Parties in the provinces in British India where the party was in power. Unable to collaborate with Gandhi, Roy stuck to his own conviction. In April 1937, his weekly *Independent India* appeared and was welcomed by left-leaning Congress leaders like Subhas Chandra Bose and Jawaharlal Nehru, but not Mahatma Gandhi. Roy became an even greater danger to the British when Bose was elected as Congress President in 1938.

IMAGE 3.1: Vladimir Lenin (left) and M.N. Roy (centre) with other delegates at the Second Congress of the Comintern in Moscow. Source: Wikipedia

On taking over as Congress President, Bose proposed a radical overhaul of Gandhi's policy of securing freedom through non-violent protests and agitations. He proposed the abandonment of non-violence as the central core of the Congress party's political line and its replacement with a policy of the pursuit of armed struggle to achieve freedom from British rule. In this regard, he urged that the Congress party be reorganised on a broad 'anti-imperialist front'. This was another way of politely saying that the party should transform itself into an Indian extension of the Comintern. Bose further stressed that the Congress needed to pursue a two-fold strategy of securing freedom from British rule by any means and establishing a socialist regime in India.

The British were very perturbed by these statements. However, they overlooked the development in the belief that Bose will not be in the next Congress presidential race due in 1939 (the term for the office of the Congress President was one year). However, Bose defied convention and went against Gandhi's expressed wishes by running for re-election in 1939 and surprisingly winning it. The British viewed this victory and the influx of communists in the Congress party as a Soviet attempt to start a violent political war inside India against British rule. The Viceroy of India Lord Linlithgow shared with Gandhi information about this plot to take over the Congress party, following which Bose was ousted from the Congress presidency within few weeks of his re-election.

The Soviet pursuit of Bose

The Soviets had been pursuing Bose since 1920 when he was 'spotted' by Indo-British communist Rajni Palme Dutt and identified by Comrade Petrov of the Comintern as a very promising recruit to push their agenda in India. Bose had declined an invitation to attend the second Comintern in Moscow in the early 1920s. The Comintern then sent Abani Mukherjee to India to pursue Bose to accept their invitation, but Bose refused to board the Soviet bus. Stalin needed a man of Bose's talent to steal the Congress party away from Gandhi and use its mass base to promote revolution through armed struggle, which would deal a death blow to the British Empire. But no one in the Soviet system was able to explain the dialectic of this argument to Bose. The task fell on one of Bose's trusted aides A.C.N. Nambiar.

IMAGE 3.2: A.C.N. Nambiar. Source: Public Domain

Nambiar was the fourth son of writer Vengayil Kunhiraman Nayanar and Arathil Kandathil Kalyani Amma. He was born in Thalasseri, Kerala, in 1896 and went to London to pursue his studies. Over there, he became influenced by the famous revolutionary

Chatto, or Virendranath Chattopadhyay, younger brother of Sarojini Naidu. He married Suhasini Chattopadhyay, the strikingly beautiful sister of Naidu and Chatto, in 1919 in Berlin. The newlywed Nambiar couple were both part of a secret circle of Indian revolutionaries in Berlin called the Champak-Chatto Berlin Committee. This circle was operated by Virendranath Chattopadhyay.

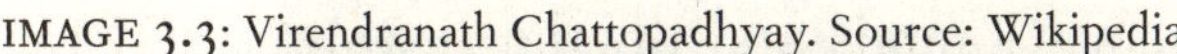
IMAGE 3.3: Virendranath Chattopadhyay. Source: Wikipedia

Meanwhile, from Berlin, Chatto went to Moscow in 1920 to attend the Second World Congress of the Comintern. There he met Roy and used his help to mobilise financial and political support for India's independence movement. Helping them closely was Mikhail Borodin, a prominent Comintern agent. Roy also introduced Chatto to Agnes Smedley, whom he intimately knew from his time in the US.

Back in December 1921 in Berlin, Chatto founded the Indian News and Information Bureau with Rash Behari Bose, who was his correspondent based in Japan. For seven years from 1921 to 1928, Chatto lived in Berlin with Agnes Smedley, who was also an agent of the Joint State Political Directorate under the Council of People's Commissars of the USSR (OGPU), the predecessor to the People's Commissariat for Internal Affairs (NKVD)/Komitet Gosudarstvennoy Bezopasnosti (KGB). Chatto remained in Berlin until 1932 as the general secretary of the League Against Imperialism and Colonial Oppression and was able to convince Nehru to affiliate the Indian National Congress with the league in 1927. The same year he accompanied Nehru to Brussels to attend a conference of the League Against Imperialism. Nehru was President of the Congress party at this point. He also became acquainted with Agnes Smedley.

Nambiar evolves into a 'key' player

During this period, Nehru, along with his father Motilal and wife Kamala, met Nambiar in Berlin. A deep and lasting friendship developed between the two men. Nambiar's elder brother Madhavan was Nehru's contemporary at Cambridge. Nehru financially supported Chatto's Indian News and Information Bureau in Berlin. Nambiar was placed in charge of it. He ran this office with help from his typist Eva Geissler, who earlier worked in Communist Party of Germany (KPD). An affair followed and Nambiar divorced his wife some years later. Suhasini studied in Moscow for quite a few years. In July 1928, Nambiar visited her in Moscow at the invitation and expense of the Soviet government. He was also a member of the KPD. Eva Geissler's sister Louise was living with Roy. The link to Moscow and the Comintern was secure. Nambiar was in their embrace.

The year 1927 was very significant for Chatto. With pressure from Roy, Willi Munzenburg, who was a member of both the Comintern and KPD, became Chatto's new mentor. He secured Chatto's admission to both KPD and League Against Imperialism. With this, Chatto finally secured an identity he had been searching for. Because of his connections with the Comintern, the KPD and the League Against Imperialism, Chatto developed a very close relationship with the Berlin-based representatives of the Soviet news agency, Telegrafnoje Agentstvo Sovietskovo Soïuza (TASS). He became a key source for TASS to secure information about the Indian revolutionary movement based in Europe. Chatto worked very closely with Z.H. Menkes and U.I. Annankova, who were both based at the office of TASS in Berlin.

It was, in fact, Chatto who formally introduced his brother-in-law, Nambiar, to Menkes through a letter of introduction dated 20 February 1930, as revealed by historian Purabi Roy. This letter also confirmed and formalised the existing financial relationship between TASS and Nambiar. What was the need for such an introduction? Was this a move to provide a legitimate justification for Nambiar's visits to the TASS office in Berlin? The GRU office also operated from the same place under TASS cover. In fact, there are declassified reports that reveal that GRU was running an 'illegal' (a non-Russian foreign national who worked for the GRU but were not on its rolls) in Berlin at that time, providing information on India. The agent was referred to simply as B. This supply of information from B was regularly passed on by Annankova to the TASS chief Yakob Doletskii in Moscow. Was Annankova the 'case officer' who ran B? Was Nambiar B?

According to the book *The Cold War: Hot Wars of the Cold War*, edited by Lori Lyn Bogle, GRU officials enjoyed the typical and transparent covers of military attaches in foreign countries. In addition, the GRU made use of the TASS cover.

The GRU's first predecessor in post-tsarist Russia was created on 21 October 1918, under the sponsorship of Leon Trotsky, who was the civilian overseer of the Red Army. It was originally known as the Registration Directorate (Registrupravlenie or RU). It was given the task of handling all military intelligence, particularly the collection of intelligence of military or political significance from sources outside the Soviet Union. The GRU operated residencies all over the world. It also ran a network of 'illegals'. During this period, the GRU was headed by Yan Berzin. Berzin served in the GRU from 1920 to 1935. Among his agents was Richard Sorge.

When Smedley left Chatto in 1928, she moved to Shanghai as a foreign correspondent for a liberal

German newspaper. Thereafter, she had a torrid affair with Sorge, Berzin's deep cover agent in the Far East. Ruth Price, the author of the most recent and extensive biography of Smedley, writes that there is very strong evidence in former Soviet archives that Smedley was indeed a spy who engaged in espionage for the Comintern and on behalf of the Soviet Union. Did Berzin order Smedley to move to Shanghai to work with Sorge as a team after she switched from OGPU to GRU? All 'illegals' recruited by the GRU from the pool of exiles in Berlin were approved by GRU's Alexander Krotokov also known as Alexander Erdberg.

With this historical evidence, no further proof is needed to infer that Nambiar was a 'fellow traveller' with the GRU. At the same time, he was extremely close to Nehru. Over the years, through the 1930s, Nehru continued to fund Nambiar's life in Europe. Both Nambiar and Chatto used their journalistic cover to spy for the USSR. After Chatto moved to Moscow in 1931, Nambiar was pretty much left alone in Berlin.

However, Nambiar's movements were also being watched by Department 1A, the German counterintelligence agency that made way to the Gestapo in April 1933. He was a foreigner with a British passport. He was a member of the KPD, and he also worked for TASS. Soon after the Nazi party came to power, Nambiar was arrested on 27 January 1933 along with a number of other Indian 'revolutionaries' and released after two months on 25 March 1933. After his release, he was deported to Prague. Was Nambiar 'turned' during his two-month detention, and did he become a 'double agent' working for both the Soviets and the Nazis? Why was he released unless he was turned? Did he continue to work for the GRU? If the GRU felt that he had been turned, they would have definitely had him liquidated. So then, could he have transitioned into an impeccable and confident double agent?

During this time in Berlin, it is unlikely that Nambiar would not have encountered Georgi Dimitrov, who was sent to Berlin by the Comintern to take charge of its central European section. Dimitrov replaced Munzenburg. The latter was a close friend of Chatto and also knew Nambiar. While Nambiar was in prison, Dimitrov was arrested by the Kripo, Nazi Germany's Criminal Police, on 9 March 1933. He was released from prison in December 1933, after which he went to Moscow via a brief sojourn in Paris. In later years, between 1935 and 1938, Dimitrov 'ran' the CPI from Moscow as the head of the Comintern.

Barely a few weeks before Nambiar's release and deportation from Berlin to Prague, Subhas Chandra Bose arrived in Vienna in the first week of March 1933. Bose and Nehru were very close friends. Bose's approach to befriending Nambiar was not a bolt from the blue. There are very strong grounds to infer that Bose was introduced to Nambiar by Nehru. As mentioned earlier, Nehru had been financially supporting Nambiar since 1927; he was a contemporary of Nambiar's brother at Cambridge. Nambiar had, in turn, been introduced to Nehru by Chatto. When Nambiar met Bose in Prague, he was possibly working for three masters: the Soviets, the Nazis and Nehru. All three of his masters had a common interest in Bose.

The Germans who were rearming after Hitler took power needed to identify potential partners in anticipation of a looming confrontation with the British. Both Captain Conrad Patzig, Abwehr chief till 1935, and his successor Admiral Wilhelm Franz Canaris succeeded in befriending Bose, and Bose became a critical part of their plan to confront the British. For this task, Nambiar was also a key component. The fact that Nambiar was back in Berlin in December 1933, albeit on a visit barely nine months after having been released from incarceration, is a valid and tested prediction of this theory.

For Nambiar, this confluence of interests of his three masters made his task simpler and also enabled him to reconcile the contradictions that were likely to arise in pursuit of such an objective. Bose needed a German interpreter who was also fluent in English. The Nazis would not permit any interpreter for this task, other than one of their own.

IMAGE 3.4: (L–R) A.C.N. Nambiar, an unknown lady, Subhas Chandra Bose, Bose's nephew and Emilie Schenkel. Source: Public Domain

A 24-year-old Austrian girl called Emilie Schenkel from a petite bourgeois background was introduced to Bose by Dr Mathur in 1934. Who was this Dr Mathur and how did he know Bose? Did Nambiar introduce Dr Mathur to Bose? Did Dr Mathur know that Schenkel's membership number in the NSF&DF (National Socialist Women's League) was E 211? This was the women's wing of the Nazi party. Was Schenkel an Abwehr agent whose mission was to honeytrap Bose? Was Nambiar aware of this, and was he a party to this plan? Did the prospect of Bose falling for a German girl also serve Nehru's purpose of tying down Bose?

Nazi interest in India's Aryan heritage

In 1928, the Deutsche Akademie created a department called Indischer Ausschuss or the India Institute. The co-founders of this department were Karl Haushofer and the Bengali nationalist Tarak Nath Das. Haushofer was the teacher and 'guru' of Hitler's deputy Rudolf Hess. Both Haushofer and Hess were members of the famous Thule Society. Das was a disciple of the revolutionary Jatin Mukherjee, founder of the Jugantar Party of Bengal and well known as Bagha Jatin.

The Deutsche Akademie's India Institute awarded scholarships to about 100 Indian students between 1929 and 1938. By the time the Nazis took power in Germany in January 1933, various German Indologists were drawing ethnocultural parallels between German warrior castes and the Vedic Kshatriyas by analysing the Bhagavad Gita with the Nordic Eddas for similarities. Two eminent

Indologists namely Jacob Hauer and Walter Wust were at the forefront of this theory. Wust was a Vedic scholar and an SS Standartenfuhrer who was close to Reichsfurher Himmler, Director of the SS's (Schutzstaffel or Paramilitary in Nazi Germany) Ahnenerbe, a pseudo-scientific organisation dedicated to discovering and propagating research about ancient Aryan ancestors of the Germans. In his 1939 book *The Aryan Warrior God*, Hauer, who was also an SS officer, portrayed the Vedic god Indra as a model for Nazi soldiers. To spread Indo-Aryan martial values within the SS, Himmler advocated regular meditation sessions according to Indian religious leaders. He also used the Bhagavad Gita to rationalise SS's crimes like the Night of the Long Knives by citing the sacralisation of terror embodied in the Gita.

Himmler was looking at connecting with an Indian leader who could convert the German theoretical identification with Vedic philosophy and spirituality into a practical partnership on the ground. Bose was a potential candidate, and his guide in Europe was Nambiar, who was also presumably working with the Nazis after his release from incarceration.

IMAGE 3.5: SS officer and Indologist Walter Wust. Source: Wikipedia

From 1937, under the orders of Himmler, the India Institute was headed by Walter Wust. The institute also became active in pro-German propaganda during the Nazi period and was incorporated into the Nazi Party/Foreign Organization (NSDAP/AO), and was instrumental in starting Nazi cells in various firms in Calcutta that were under German control. It also funded German teachers in Calcutta who taught German to Indian students who wanted to go to Germany. Two of these were Nazi party members, namely Horst Pohle and Alfred Werfull. They allegedly established powerful spy rings in and around Calcutta and Benares. Among other Indians closely associated with the institute were Benoy Kumar Sarkar, an admirer and supporter of the Nazis, and Bose's nephew Ashok Bose.

The historian Purabi Roy has argued that Nambiar introduced Bose to TASS representatives in Berlin upon his return in 1933. The office was ostensibly run by Menkes and Annankova. The Soviets were very pleased.

The Nazis gave Bose a long rope in pursuing his leftist agenda. This pursuit brought a whole range of people—Indian origin revolutionaries, anti-British individuals and Soviet illegals—to the knowledge of both the Abwehr and the Kripo. At the same time, the pressure was put on Bose by Schenkel to formalise their relationship. Such a step would, however, have spelt the death knell for Bose's continuation as a serious political figure in the struggle for independence. What was he to do? Faced with this quandary, Bose returned to India in early 1936.

But the lure of Schenkel was very powerful, so Bose was back in Badgastein in November 1937. This time he was President-elect of the Congress party. Nambiar was witness to the unconventional marriage ceremony, even by Nazi standards, of Bose and Schenkel on 26 December 1937 at Badgastein. Bose also used this time in Germany to complete his book *An Indian Pilgrim*, in which he advocated the superiority of armed struggle over non-violence. There was now a public tilt in Bose's favour on the Comintern line. Nambiar's co-brother Roy was admitted into the Congress in December 1936 along with several hundred leftists, as has been revealed earlier in this chapter.

Bose's red shadow

In the presidential elections held on 29 January 1939, Bose defeated Gandhi's candidate P. Sitaramayya by over 200 votes. Nehru sided with Gandhi. Despite the unexpected victory helped by left support, Bose couldn't last long in his second term as Congress President. He faced strident opposition from Gandhi and soon resigned on 29 April 1939.

Did Nehru reveal to Gandhi all the secrets of Bose's life in Germany? Did Nambiar have a role to play in bringing all these facts to Nehru? With this, did Nambiar thwart the Comintern's plan to take over the Congress party? Did Nambiar finally prove his new unswerving loyalty to the Nazis who didn't want to lose Bose to the Soviets?

Were the Soviets disappointed with Bose's dethronement? Did they fear that Bose's romantic involvement with Schenkel would cause him to fall into a Nazi embrace? Did the Soviet-Nazi pact of 1939 present a dilemma to the Soviets about the future moves of Bose? On 4 July 1939, Bose corresponded with Schenkel and had plans to visit her in Germany in August or September that year. However, Hitler's invasion of Poland on 1 September 1939 put paid to all such plans. Bose was grief-stricken.

There are unsubstantiated reports that if Bose had not been arrested for seditious speeches in July 1940, he would have been escorted to Moscow by Punjab Kirti Party leader Achhar Singh Chhina to meet Stalin. It is acknowledged in certain left-wing circles in India that after Bose's arrest in July 1940, Chhina went by himself to see Stalin and secured promises of continuing Soviet help to Bose. On his return, Chhina is reported to have submitted a written report to the Politburo of the CPI. The existence of this document is neither confirmed nor denied. It is within this backdrop—the Nazi-Soviet pact of 1939 and the confluence of interest in Bose—that a joint Abwehr-GRU operation spirited Bose out of house arrest in Calcutta via Kabul and Moscow. Soviet archival records about what Bose did and whom he met while he was in Moscow on 23–31 March 1941 remain classified.

Bose's activities and meetings in Moscow during this brief interregnum are a matter of pure speculation. This information is also classified in Soviet-era archives in Russia. When Bose arrived in Berlin via

Moscow in April 1941, adequate groundwork had already been done to label and stigmatise Bose as a left-wing pro-Soviet agent of the Comintern. Was this disinformation spread by the GRU so that the Nazis would expel Bose back into the USSR? The GRU had not reckoned with the important role that the Nazis had earmarked for Bose. Not only were they expecting him to enlist in the Wehrmacht the 40,000 Indian prisoners of war (POWs) captured by Field Marshall Rommel's Afrika Corps, but Himmler also needed him to orchestrate the symbiosis between the Nazi ideology and what they perceived as the Indo-Aryan esotericism.

Chapter 4

The British Plan Their Moves in Kashmir

Second World War reveals cracks in British control over India

The provincial elections in 11 key provinces of British India in the winter of 1936–1937 under the Government of India Act, 1935, saw the Congress party emerging victorious in 8 provinces. The All-India Muslim League was nowhere in the reckoning. With Bose taking over as Congress President in 1938, all thanks to the support from left-leaning fresh members of the Congress party, the stage was set for a major upset to the British Raj. Bose's unprecedented re-election in 1939 further alarmed the British.

Admittedly, around this time the CPI was under the vice-like grip of the Comintern. It had been banned in India from 1934 to 1938. When Comintern General Secretary Georgi Dimitrov propounded his thesis of a popular front against fascism, the Congress party received an influx of communists led by Roy. Famous communists like Dinkar Mehta, Sajjad Zaheer, Soli Batliwala and E.M.S. Namboodiripad joined the Congress during this time. Within the party, they gravitated towards a caucus called the Congress Socialist Party.

However, Bose resigned from the presidency on 29 April 1939 after being outmanoeuvred by Gandhi. In order to consolidate left forces who had been shell shocked with his resignation from the presidency, Bose formed another caucus within the Congress party called the Forward Bloc on 3 May 1939 at Unnao in the United Provinces (present-day Uttar Pradesh).

On 23 August 1939, Nazi Germany and Soviet Russia signed a no-war pact. A week after, on 1 September 1939, the Second World War began. The British were under siege, as was their empire. The empire could not be defended without the formal and active participation of the Government of India. All eight Congress ministries from the key provinces of British India resigned in October and November 1939 in protest against Viceroy Lord Linlithgow's unilateral declaration of war against the Axis powers in September 1939. The Congress high command was not taken into confidence. Other right-wing political parties like the Hindu Mahasabha and the All-India Muslim League supported Linlithgow's actions. The CPI was banned again, but on 2 October 1939, it launched an anti-war strike involving 90,000 workers engaged in war efforts. Mass arrests of communists began to take place.

The British now feared and distrusted what appeared to be a left-dominated Congress party infested with the beliefs of Subhas Chandra Bose. The British control and domination over India began to weaken. Recruitment into the Indian Army had to be stepped up. The Army had only 200,000 troops in 1939, which was sufficient to keep India under British rule and safe from Indian revolutionaries. In order to step up recruitment and raise its strength to one million men, as well as mobilise over 14 million industrial workers to work in factories producing war materials, political opposition to British rule within the massive Congress party had to be neutralised and its widespread appeal diluted.

The impetuousness of the Congress leadership in hastily tendering their resignations led to their losing control over the NWFP, where they were in power. Had the Congress retained power there till 1947—which they could have, easily—the outcome of Partition would have been very different.

Meanwhile, following the political vacuum thus created, disparate groups hankered for power and the idea of the separation of India into two separate homelands for Muslims and Hindu began to take shape. The idea was vividly expressed by Mohammed Ali Jinnah in an article in a London weekly *Time and Tide* on 9 March 1940. The publication of this article was followed by the momentous Lahore Resolution of the All-India Muslim League on 24 March 1940 wherein the first formal demand for Pakistan was made.

The resignation of the Congress ministries, the creation of two caucuses within the Congress party, the Nazi-Soviet no-war pact and the start of the Second World War convinced Linlithgow that a partition of the country would perhaps weaken the political opposition to British rule. Jinnah appeared a 'reliable and pliable' ally.

Bose was arrested in July 1940, soon after a ban was imposed on the Forward Bloc on 23 June 1940 following its first conclave. He escaped from Calcutta to Germany via Kabul and Moscow in January 1941.

By May 1941, almost 20,000 leftists had been jailed in detention camps in Deoli, Rajputana and Hooghly under the Defence of India Rules.

The Nazi-Soviet no-war pact of August 1939 collapsed with the launch of Operation Barbarossa on 22 June 1941. This was the Nazi invasion of the Soviet Union.

This had a direct impact on the communist agitation in India. The Comintern declared that this was a transformation of the war. However, it took some time for the interned CPI leadership in Deoli jail to come out openly in support of the Government of India. In December 1941, the CPI leadership in Deoli jail came out with a 'Jail Document' in which they supported the British war effort without linking it to their demand for independence. The new party line was enunciated by the CPI General Secretary P.C. Joshi, who argued that India would secure freedom in the course of supporting the war effort. This was at variance with the Congress line and also that of Bose's, who was in Germany.

Operation Barbarossa resulted in Britain and the Soviet Union seeking comfort in each other's company. The Anglo-Soviet Agreement of July 1941 was signed by virtue of which Britain and the Soviet Union would assist each other in fighting Germany and would not seek a separate peace.

This agreement was soon superseded by the Anglo-Soviet Treaty signed in London on 26 May 1942. The treaty established a politico-military alliance between the Soviet Union and the British Empire, including India. The military alliance was to last till the end of the Second World War. The political part of the treaty was to last till 1962. Joseph Stalin dissolved the Comintern in July 1943 in order not to antagonise the US and Britain, who were his military allies.

Impact on Maharaja Hari Singh's Kashmir

Meanwhile, within the Valley, political unrest increased after the declaration of the Pakistan Resolution in Lahore in 1940. The Lahore Resolution, presented by A.K. Fazlul Haq at the three-day general session of the All-India Muslim League in Lahore on 22–24 March 1940, is popularly known as the Pakistan Resolution because it called for independent states based on religion. The Anglo-Soviet pacts made during the Second World War and Stalin's subsequent disbandment of the Comintern provided the Government of India some respite from the perceived Soviet threat to the state of Kashmir. Hari Singh, anticipating the inevitable departure of the British from the subcontinent, needed to broaden his popular support. He sought to do this by appointing one Muslim and one Hindu member of the legislative assembly as ministers in his government. That he even considered doing this is a reflection of how fast socio-religious equations were changing in the state and how inadequate the state forces were in quelling any Muslim uprisings. Hari Singh chose Mirza Afzal Beg, the deputy leader of the National Conference and a close associate of Abdullah, as Minister of Public Works and Municipalities. Wazir Ganga Ram was the Hindu minister chosen by the Maharaja.

Beg's collaboration with the Maharaja undoubtedly reflected Abdullah's political craftiness and his excellent sense of timing.

The Poonch imbroglio

The passing of the Pakistan Resolution in Lahore in March 1940 coincided with important developments in Poonch, which was a feudatory part of Hari Singh's kingdom of Jammu and Kashmir. Way back in 1827, Maharaja Ranjit Singh appointed Raja Dhyan Singh, Gulab Singh's brother, as the Raja of Poonch. Gulab Singh was appointed the Raja of Jammu. After the death of Maharaja Ranjit Singh in 1839, Dhyan Singh was assassinated in Lahore in the September 1843 coup d'état of the Sikh Emperor Sher Singh. It is speculated that Gulab Singh had a role to play in this event. Thereafter, Poonch was confiscated by the Sikh Empire on the grounds of Raja Dhyan Singh's rebellion. Poonch was handed over to Faiz Talib Khan of Rajouri and after the signing of the Treaty of Amritsar, it was transferred to Maharaja Gulab Singh by the British. He, in turn, restored Poonch to Jawahir Singh, the eldest surviving son of Dhyan Singh, albeit with the reduced status of a *jagir*, a feudal land grant. Gulab Singh had cleverly managed to neutralise potential opposition he and his descendants would have faced from his family. The rumoured circumstantial evidence of Gulab Singh's role in the death of his brother Dhyan Singh and the demotion of Poonch to a *jagir* angered Dhyan Singh's clansmen led by Jawahir Singh and his younger brother, Moti Singh. They petitioned the British, their trusted ally who did not want to annoy Gulab Singh. In 1852, the arbitrator Sir Frederick Currie, the British Resident in Lahore, ruled that Gulab Singh was indeed the suzerain, or the feudal overlord, of Poonch. The *jagir* was further subdivided into Jawahir Singh's two-thirds share and the remaining one-third of Moti Singh's. Later on, in 1859, Maharaja Ranbir Singh and the British levelled a charge of 'treacherous conspiracy' against Jawahir Singh and dispossessed him of his rightful share. This left Moti Singh, his son Baldev Singh and grandson Jagat Dev Singh with a much-truncated *jagir*. The descendants of Raja Dhyan Singh were marginalised by those of his brother Gulab Singh's, and this intergenerational bitterness continued into the era of Hari Singh.

When a beleaguered Maharaja Pratap Singh sought to resist the combined pressure of Raja Amar Singh and his British masters to impose Hari Singh as the heir to the throne, he turned to his marginalised second cousin's nephew Jagat Dev Singh and adopted him as his son and heir. Jagat performed the last rites of Maharaja Pratap Singh in 1925 and became the Raja of Poonch in 1928. Hari Singh, however, continued the policy of marginalisation of the *jagir* and imposed a *sanad*, or a land deed, on Jagat, which further encroached on Jagat's administration. This effectively established a diarchy. Hari Singh appointed a Resident Administrator, and more officials were loaned from the state, leaving Raja Jagat Dev Singh's jurisdiction to handle only petty cases. All serious crimes were referred to the courts in Srinagar. The powers of the Raja of Poonch were completely diminished, and the throne lost its prestige as well as power.

With the British and the Maharaja both against the Raja of Poonch, and with the residual part of the state being inconsequential because the Maharaja imposed heavy taxes, the choice before Raja Jagat Dev Singh was limited. It can be argued that with the rising powers of the Muslim Conference and the National Conference, the clouds of war in Europe and the growing communal divide in the rest of India, the Raja had only one weapon to use against the enemies of his family—the mobilisation and militarisation of the Muslim subjects of the state. Muslims constituted 90 per cent of Poonch's population; they were ethnically different from the Muslims in the larger Kashmir Valley and also spoke Punjabi. Over 30,000 men from Poonch served in the Indian Army in the First World War; they were enlisted as 'Punjabi *Mussalmans*' and were admitted into the Punjab Regiment. In the Second World War, over 60,000 men from Poonch served in the Indian Army and formed the nucleus of the revolt against the Maharaja in 1947. Raja Jagat Dev Singh feared that Maharaja Hari Singh would leave no stone unturned to completely usurp his power. His only option now was to fan communal unrest and encourage a Muslim revolt against the Maharaja. However, the Muslim population needed a leader and Raja Jagat Dev Singh thought Muhammad Ibrahim Khan, the son of his carpenter, was a perfect fit. He sent the young man to Lahore to finish his graduation and then sent him to London to study law. Khan obtained a bar-at-law degree from Lincoln's Inn and became Raja Jagat Dev

Singh's agent provocateur against the Maharaja. After returning to India in 1943, Khan started his career as a Public Prosecutor in Mirpur.

Unfortunately, Raja Jagat Dev Singh died under mysterious circumstances in 1940, and his wife was prevented from taking control of the *jagir* in the name of their minor son, Ratan Dev Singh. She eventually fled to Nepal with her son and two daughters. The *jagir* came under the direct control of Hari Singh, which agitated Khan, who was then studying in London. He planned to avenge the death of his benefactor and the marginalisation of his benefactor's descendants, and in the process, he also wanted to advance the interests of Poonch's Muslim majority, who would now come under the direct rule of the Maharaja. Hari Singh, sticking to the tradition of his predecessors to marginalise surviving members of Dhyan Singh's family, unwittingly created what was going to be, in 1947, the pivot for the multi-pronged attack on Hari Singh's rule and state. The Poonch family was not the only problem that was going to grow into terrifying proportions.

William Brown: the British agent provocateur

As mentioned in Chapter 2, in 1935, Hari Singh's attitude prompted the British to take over the Gilgit Wazarat on a 60 year lease. Gilgit was the last outpost of British India before the landmass of Jammu and Kashmir merged with Sinkiang. To the south of Gilgit flowed the mighty Indus, meandering westward towards Punjab. To the north of Gilgit lay the Karakoram range.

Of the eight known passes between Central Asia and the subcontinent, six lay within a week's march from Gilgit. From 1935, the leased region of the Gilgit Wazarat was treated as part of British India and, along with the Gilgit Agency, was administered by a Political Agent who reported to the Resident in Srinagar, who, in turn, reported to the Viceroy's office in Delhi. As a result, the kingdoms of Chitral, Hunza, Nagar Haveli, Puniyal, Chilas Yasin, Yashkoman and Koh-e-Khizr, all vassals in name of the Maharaja of Kashmir, were under direct British rule. The newly leased territory was merged with the Gilgit Agency and no longer referred to as a Wazarat. The Maharaja was out of this territory.

The defeats that the Soviets suffered at the hands of the Nazis in 1942 led Shicai to switch his allegiance to the KMT, because of which he expelled all Soviet technicians and military personnel from Sinkiang. The KMT government of China dispatched Ma Bu-fang to Sinkiang at the head of a large force. He reintegrated Sinkiang with the rest of China by building key roads linking Qinghai with Sinkiang. On 17 September 1942, Shicai arrested some members of the Communist Party of China (CPC) who were active in the province because of Soviet presence. Shicai had these cadres arrested and executed in 1943. Among those executed was Mao Tse-min, brother of Chinese Communist Party (CCP) boss Mao Tse-tung. As a reward, Shicai was absorbed into the KMT and appointed head of the party's Sinkiang branch. He in turn opened the doors for the KMT cadres to take root in the province.

All of these significant developments did not go undetected in New Delhi. The Americans, the British, the Germans and the Russians were all engaged in a bitter race to be the first to master the power of the atom. News about the discovery of uranium mining by the Soviets, in Sinkiang, sent New Delhi into a tizzy. The Government of India was ordered, under instructions from Whitehall, to build up a network of local couriers to retrieve goods and materials from Kashgar and carry them across the border to Gilgit. In effect, the samples of uranium, beryllium and other ores being mined by the Soviets had to be transported back to India for further transhipment to the US. This was necessary to continually assess Soviet success in building the bomb.

IMAGE 4.1: Major William Brown, Indian Army. Source: Wikimedia Commons

In pursuit of these aims, the British posted a Pashto-speaking Indian Army officer called Lieutenant William Brown to the Gilgit Agency in early 1943. Brown was appointed adjutant to the Gilgit Scouts and reported to Lieutenant Colonel E.H. Cobb, who wore two hats. Cobb not only was the Commanding Officer of the scouts but he was also the Political Agent of the entire Gilgit Agency and in turn reported to the Resident in Srinagar. Brown spent the next three years in this region. He learned Pashto at Peshawar while serving with the South Waziristan Scouts in 1942–1943. After his promotion to Captain, he was appointed as the Assistant Political Agent of Chilas, which is only 135 kilometres from Gilgit. Brown devoted himself to travelling throughout the Gilgit Agency, recruiting agents, establishing networks and, in the process, gaining invaluable local knowledge. He learned Shina, the dialect of the region, as well as a working knowledge of Burushaski, the language of Hunza. Brown also established close ties with the Raja of Nagar Haveli, Raja Muzaffar-ul-Din Shah, and the ruler of Chitral, the Mir of Hunza, the Raja of Yasin and the Raja of Puniyal.

Contemporaneous to Brown's Gilgit Agency posting, the US government secured permission to open a Consulate in Tihwa, the capital of Sinkiang, to coincide with the departure of the Soviets from Sinkiang and Shicai's embrace of the KMT. The Tihwa mission was opened by Consul Edmund Clubb in March 1943. There is circumstantial evidence to point to the fact that Clubb had to hand over uranium and beryllium ore samples to a courier network controlled or influenced by Brown. The 'package' would then be transhipped via Kashgar to Gilgit. The defection of Shicai to the KMT once again permitted trade to resume between the Gilgit Agency and Sinkiang. A protocol was signed by the governments of India and Sinkiang to permit trade carried through pack animals. This trade was monopolised by two British Indian firms: Central Asian Trading Company and Pekin Syndicate Ltd. Brown's mandate was to infiltrate these two companies with his own agents and carry the ores undercover through these two legitimate transportation services.

The rebellion in Sinkiang

With the defeat of the German Army on the eastern front in the summer of 1944, a wily Shicai quickly moved in to rebuild bridges with the Soviets at the expense of the KMT. He engineered the arrest of a number of KMT cadres in Tihwa and in confidence wrote to Stalin proposing the absorption of Sinkiang by the Soviet Union as the 18th Soviet Socialistic Republic of the USSR. The proposal included a proviso for Shicai to be the ruler of the new Soviet Republic. Stalin rejected Shicai's proposal and sent a confidential letter to KMT Generalissimo Chiang Kai-shek. The result was that Shicai was removed from his post and recalled to Chungking and banished to a low-level bureaucratic post.

However, the Soviets took advantage of the ensuing power vacuum and instigated the Turkic-origin inhabitants of Sinkiang's Ili region to revolt against the KMT. The long Soviet shadow began to recast over Sinkiang. By November 1944, direct Soviet support enabled the rebels to 'liberate' three districts of northern Sinkiang. The ethnic Chinese population of these districts was reduced by massacres and expulsion. The rebel forces were called the East Turkestan Army and consisted of 60,000 troops. The Red Army units that supported these troops numbered 500 officers and 2,000 soldiers. A further detachment of 20,000 Kazakh horsemen was under the command of one Osman Bator. A ceasefire was declared in 1946. The second East Turkestan Republic controlled Ili in northern Sinkiang and the KMT controlled Tihwa and the rest of Sinkiang.

The British move to counter the fallout of Bose's escape

Bose escaped from house arrest in Calcutta on the night of 16 January 1941 intending to reach Berlin via Moscow. On 17 February 1941, Hitler ordered the operations staff of the High Command of the Nazi German Armed Forces, OKW (Oberkommando der Wehrmacht), to plan the invasion of India via the Soviet Union and Afghanistan. OKW was a military general staff of the Third Reich that coordinated the efforts of the German Army, Navy and Air Force. Their cypher traffic communicated via the Enigma machine was compromised by the British by 1941. The official order for the planned invasion of India was issued under 'OKW/WEStb/L No. 44180/41 gk'.

By all accounts, these were preliminary plans to prepare for any British attempts to directly threaten or harm Germany from India. Furthermore, Operation Orient, or Fall Orient, was the code name of a Nazi operation that sought to link up with the Japanese at longitude 70° E in India. This operation was to be initiated after the capture of the Caucasus and the collapse of resistance in the Soviet Union.

After the collapse of Singapore on 15 February 1942, the defection of 40,000 Indian POWs to Japanese forces under the leadership of Captain Mohan Singh and the recruitment of 3,000 Indian POWs in Germany by Subhas Chandra Bose, the British were distraught that they could no longer rely on the loyalty of Indian troops if the war came to India's western borders.

Case Blue, or Fall Bleu, was a joint military offensive of the German Army and Air Force in southern Russia from 28 June to 24 November 1942. The operation was a continuation of the previous year's Operation Barbarossa under which the Nazis invaded the Soviet Union. The British were very concerned about the possibility of German forces moving to the south and east and linking up with Japanese forces in India, then advancing towards Burma. However, the Red Army defeated the Germans at Stalingrad following operations Uranus and Little Saturn. This defeat forced the Germans to retreat from the Caucasus and that marked the end of a direct German threat to India.

Most historians are unaware that the fallout of the defections of Indian POWs in Germany and Singapore had a major impact on the Government of India. Added to this were the Quit India Movement of 1942 and the potential threat from the radicalised labour force involved in the war effort. Sir George Cunningham, one of the key civil servants in the Government of India, began to plan since 1944 for the partition of India and the transfer of power. Blessed by Cunningham, who was serving his second term as the Governor of NWFP, a frontier committee was formed under Lieutenant General Sir Francis Tucker. Its task was to recommend a new frontier policy. This committee recommended withdrawing regular Indian Army troops from the Razmak, Wana and Khyber Pass garrisons and replacing them with scouts and *khassadars* (tribal levies). Both Cunningham and Sir Olaf Caroe supported the immediate implementation of these recommendations. The immediate effect of this was the removal of all Hindu and Sikh army officers and soldiers from the NWFP and having the northern frontiers of India defended by the Muslim-staffed Frontier Scouts and Frontier Constabulary.

IMAGE 4.2: Sir Claude Auchinleck as Commander-in-Chief of the Indian Army. Source: Wikipedia

In 1944, the Indian Army's Khojak Brigade on the Baluchistan frontier was disbanded. In March 1945, the Indian Army's Tal Brigade was disbanded and some of its units were assigned to the Kohat Brigade. In April 1946, the Commander-in-Chief (C-in-C) of the Indian Army, Field Marshal Sir Claude Auchinleck, presided over a high-level conference at Peshawar. It was attended by the Governor of NWFP, Sir George Cunningham, the Political Agent to the Governor of Baluchistan, the British Consul at Kabul and senior military and civil officers. A unanimous decision was reached to replace regular troops in all tribal areas with scouts and *khassadars*. It was to be a gradual withdrawal in five phases and to be completed over two years. It was against this background that the Pishin Scouts were raised. A decision was also made to raise Central Waziristan Scouts and to retrain the Malakand Battalion. The Khyber Rifles was re-raised on 26 April 1946. The recruiting pool was to be drawn from the wartime-raised Afridi Battalion. Lieutenant Colonel Muhammad Sharif Khan, aka Sharifo (5/10 Baluch Regiment), was appointed the Commandant of the Khyber Rifles. *Khassadars* were to be trained and disciplined to make them a reliable partner of the scouts. To achieve this objective, a new position called District Officer was created in 1946 to take charge of *khassadars*. In North Waziristan, for instance, about 2,000 *khassadars* were put under the command of the new District Officer Frank Leeson.

Osman Bator works for the CIA

Osman Bator, who was perhaps America's first atomic spy, began keeping a long vigil on the Soviet activities in Altai in Sinkiang, primarily as an agent run by Clubb, and after him by his successor John Paxton. After Hiroshima and Nagasaki, the greatest atomic secret was that the US was fighting to maintain a global monopoly on the supply of uranium. The main aim of that monopoly was to keep uranium out of the Soviet's reach. The existing courier network between Sinkiang and the Gilgit Agency run by Brown needed to be upgraded to an espionage network that would be able to use and transmit the flow of intelligence being generated by Osman Bator's Uyghurs and Kazakhs. This intelligence was going to waste as the US Consulate in Tihwa was a one-man operation run by John Paxton. The consular staff needed to be increased and a covert officer appointed to serve under Paxton in Tihwa.

In 1944, the US and Britain signed the top-secret '1944 Hyde Park Agreement'. The signatories were Prime Minister Churchill and President Roosevelt. For some strange reason, the US copy of this classified document was lost in Roosevelt's papers after his death in 1945. Unaware of this top-secret Anglo-US agreement, the US Senate and the House of Representatives passed the Atomic Energy Act of 1946, aka McMahon Act, which became law on 1 August 1946. It restricted access to nuclear information to other countries and left Britain out of the loop. For Britain, therefore, it became vital to spy on what developments were taking place in Sinkiang, Soviet Tajikistan and Soviet Kazakhstan, and the relationship that various entities established in these areas shared with the uranium mines in the Koktogai Valley, which was also in the same region. This was vital for Britain if it wanted to make the atom bomb using its own resources and skills.

Tube Alloys Liaison

The British painstakingly began to create the means to build their own independent nuclear deterrent. The entire exercise was shrouded in layers of secrecy and deniability.

IMAGE 4.3: Commander Eric Welsh in a meeting with Samuel Gouldsmith, Fred Wardenburg and Rupert Cecil. Source: Wikipedia

In his book *Spying on the Nuclear Bear*, Michael S. Goodman recounts the riveting tale about how Britain literally clawed its way into the nuclear club. A British naval officer, Commander Eric Welsh moved to MI6, the Foreign Intelligence Service of the UK, during the Second World War and was engaged in atomic espionage against the Nazis. After the end of the war in Europe in May 1945, Welsh took charge of a classified unit within MI6 called Tube Alloys Liaison (TAL) because the British nuclear programme was assigned the code name Tube Alloys Project. The acronym TAL was also used alternatively and interchangeably as Technical Atomic Liaison whenever needed. Within the extremely secret MI6, TAL was perhaps its most clandestine aspect and was so under the radar that even operational MI6 officers had only the vaguest of vague notions about its existence on the fourth floor of Shell-Mex House in London. TAL had its own budget and a direct line to the head of MI6 known as 'C'. Welsh followed his intuition, which frequently gave rise to hunches that he pursued assiduously.

The need for the services of a top-secret outfit like TAL arose because the nuclear weapons that were dropped on Hiroshima and Nagasaki were perhaps the most significant event of the Second World War. The fact that Britain did not have the bomb or the know-how to build it made the country extremely vulnerable to these new weapons. Because of Britain's relative geographical proximity to the Soviet Union, it needed nuclear deterrence to ensure protection against future Soviet attacks. TAL's mandate was to spy on the Soviet Union's nuclear programme so that Britain would not be caught on the wrong foot.

IMAGE 4.4: Commander Eric Welsh (centre) at German experimental nuclear pile in Haigerloch. Source: Wikipedia

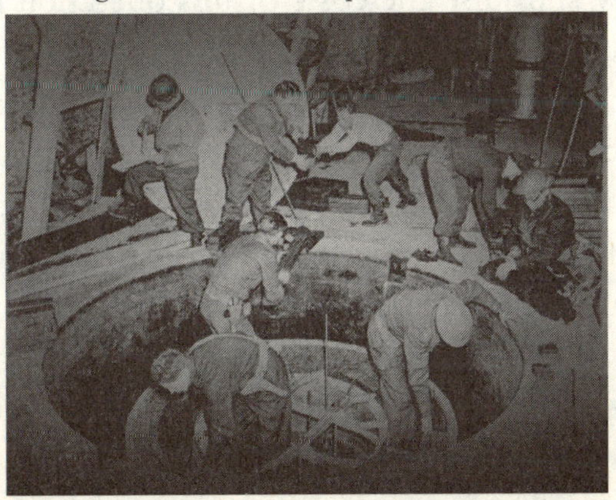

TAL was endowed with its own budget and Welsh could select intelligence targets that were potential sources of acquiring information on nuclear matters. Fortunately for the British, the Soviet nuclear-related activity was concentrated in the Sinkiang-Kazakhstan area that bordered the Gilgit Agency. They had been savvy enough to bring this region directly under the control of New Delhi since 1935. It was logistically much easier to cross an adjacent border and undertake espionage. The British had already developed the practice of espionage and sabotage into fine art in occupied Europe during the Second World War.

The complexity and gravity of the developments required Welsh to take direct control over Brown's courier network in 1945 after he became the head of TAL. Welsh knew that the Gilgit operation was going to be crucial in Britain's quest for the atomic bomb. The remit of the operation had to be expanded and more data needed to be generated from what was clearly emerging as the site of the Soviet nuclear explosion. This was at Semipalatinsk in Soviet Kazakhstan bordering Sinkiang. If Britain could share this data with the US, it could not only subsidise the costs of this operation but also enable it to continuously strengthen its access to the US nuclear weapons programme. The Semipalatinsk test site, about 150 kilometres west of Semey, was the anvil on which the Soviet Union forged its nuclear arsenal.

Monitoring seismic and acoustic activity at Semipalatinsk became a top priority for Welsh. Robert Oppenheimer, the head of the Manhattan Project that built the US nuclear bomb, doubted that the US will detect the debris from a Soviet nuclear test because of the distances involved. Therefore, the British exercise out of India became perhaps the only accurate scientific assessment of whether or not the Soviets conducted a nuclear test. It also had to be highly secret and deniable as it was located in an area the British would have to shortly vacate both legally and physically. The trick was to retain control despite the ongoing process of partition and the inevitable withdrawal from India.

Welsh manoeuvred to install Lieutenant Colonel Roger Bacon as the Political Agent in Gilgit. Bacon was an astute officer of the Indian Army who had been co-opted into the IPS. Welsh gave Bacon the additional undercover mandate to construct and commission a seismic monitoring station to monitor seismic changes occurring at Semipalatinsk in the run-up to the actual test. This station's records are still classified. Its code name was Stowage. It was established in the Gilgit Agency close to the Indus River and lay within the shadow of the Hindu Kush Mountain range. This station was closest to Semipalatinsk, and it generated a daily output that was telegraphed to the US Coast and Geodetic Survey and then to AFOAT-I, the United States Air Force (USAF) agency responsible for monitoring Soviet nuclear tests. Because of its proximity to Semipalatinsk, Stowage was always the first to receive the signal from a test. Further, Bacon also commissioned two acoustic stations in the Gilgit Agency codenamed Beaver and Tagday.

All three of these stations in the Gilgit Agency were to collect nuclear debris after the explosion. Over a period of 10 years starting in 1946, these three stations were collecting at their peak up to four filters worth of material a day, which were flown by a squadron of 20 Avro Lincoln aircraft from Chaklala airbase in Rawalpindi directly to Royal Air Force (RAF) Harwell in Oxfordshire, UK, for radiochemical analysis by a team led by Dr Frank Morgan. Morgan was, perhaps, Britain's pre-eminent radiochemist. The RAF also operated the Chaklala-based Lincoln bombers and a squadron of converted Halifax bombers for debris collection flights out of both Chaklala and Risalpur in NWFP to coincide with any blasts at Semipalatinsk. A part of this detachment of aircraft was also used for aerial photographic reconnaissance over different nuclear-related sites of interest in the Soviet Union.

IMAGE 4.5: Handley Page Halifax B III bomber showing the later rectangular fins and Bristol Hercules radial engines. Source: Wikipedia

The Halifax bombers were the A7 version, which had been converted for special operations. RAF Squadron No. 298 was relocated to India for this purpose. This squadron was part of the 10 'Special Duties-S.O.E. Squadrons' aka 'Dark of the Moon' squadrons operated by MI6. Under its Commanding Officer Wing Commander W.G. Gardiner, this squadron started operating in India in July 1945. One flight was based at RAF Chaklala from 9 December 1945. A second flight was based at RAF Risalpur, NWFP, from 27 July 1946. The main and third flight was rotated between RAF Stations Raipur, Akyab, Alipore, Negombo, Meiktila and Baroda to confuse anyone tracking the whereabouts of this squadron. Finally, on 24 July 1946, Squadron No. 298 was transferred to RAF Mauripur in Karachi. Curiously the squadron at RAF Mauripur was officially disbanded on 21 December 1946. There are no official records available as to what happened to its 20 Halifax aircraft and their pilots. It is as if they never existed. The entire squadron, ground staff and auxiliary support all went 'dark'.

IMAGE 4.6: Side profile of a converted Halifax bomber. Source: Public Domain

The significance of these activities is not that they happened, but that they happened so close to one another. The Soviet test site at Semipalatinsk and the Soviet uranium ore processing site in Tajikistan were near the British airfields in Chaklala and Risalpur. This also underscored how critical Pakistan was in Britain's scheme of things. With the prospect of partition looming, Britain moved to secure its nuclear dream. The Lincoln and Halifax aircraft were neither limited by service ceiling nor range and were even able to cover distances north and north-west of Semipalatinsk. Thus Bacon's 'nuclear monitoring empire' became a vital cog in the British quest to make the atom bomb.

These three monitoring stations in the Gilgit Agency were very important for the British and remained so until 1956. First, they provided direct evidence of the kind of weapons the Soviets were testing. Second, this resource facilitated a much-valued technical dialogue between the British and the Americans, which was necessary if Britain was to remain in the hunt for the bomb. Third, they provided scientific indications that were vital for the development of Britain's own atomic weapons.

The Chaklala and Risalpur airbases provided a regular stream of photographic intelligence, which was the second vital component of this exercise. The debris collected during actual and practice tests added to the intelligence being studied and analysed.

Finally, the human intelligence (HUMINT) resources of Bacon and Brown out of Gilgit, Chitral and Hunza provided the much-needed real-time intelligence to complete the picture.

IMAGE 4.7: RAF aircrew in summer uniform in NWFP. Source: Public Domain

The invaluable role of aerial intelligence

British Prime Minister Clement Richard Attlee formed a secret Gen 163 Cabinet committee on 8 January 1947. This committee consisted of six cabinet ministers, and they unanimously decided that Britain needed the bomb to maintain its position in world politics. This showed how important both the Gilgit Agency and Pakistan were to the British. They had to ensure that the Gilgit Agency remained under their direct control. The British only got their bomb in 1952.

The key factor in the immense importance of Stowage and its sister stations Beaver and Tagday was their proximity to the Semipalatinsk test site. The fact that RAF aircraft stationed at Risalpur and Rawalpindi were within 500 miles of the test site and brought back excellent reconnaissance photographs made the continued existence of the Gilgit Agency and Pakistan vital aspects of British national interests and security. Britain had no nuclear deterrence and this was the only way they were going to get it.

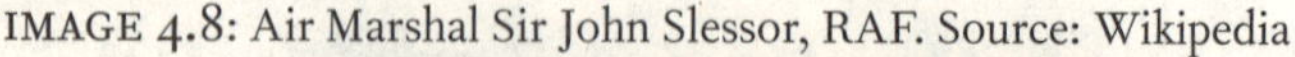
IMAGE 4.8: Air Marshal Sir John Slessor, RAF. Source: Wikipedia

Adequate aerial reconnaissance was one of the key aspects of the RAF's exercise. For this, Welsh selected, with the help of India-born Air Chief Marshal John Slessor, a mercurial Australian aviator called Sidney Cotton.

Cotton was originally recruited by MI6 in 1939 to undertake clandestine aerial reconnaissance over Nazi Germany. Soon, he wore a dual hat and was appointed Squadron Leader on 22 September 1939 and headed the newly created RAF 1 Photographic Development Unit based out of Heston airfield in England. He undertook pioneering work in aerial reconnaissance first in the early days and later throughout the war.

In 1940, Slessor, an Air Commodore then, conceived of Operation Pike, which was a strategic bombing plan against the Soviet Union by the Anglo-French alliance. Despite the Soviet's neutrality during the first two years of the Second World War, the British and French concluded that the Soviet-German pact made Stalin an accomplice of Hitler. Operation Pike was designed to inflict critical damage to the Soviet oil industry and cause the collapse of Soviet power.

In the first phase of Operation Pike, the RAF flew secret aerial reconnaissance flights inside the Soviet Union using high-altitude, high-speed stereoscopic photography developed by Cotton. Cotton himself flew many of these flights. These flights were run by MI6 from RAF Habbaniya in Iraq. The crowning glory of these missions came on 30 March 1940 when Cotton flew a Lockheed Model 14 Super Electra over the mountains of south-east Kurdistan in Iranian airspace, across the coast of the Caspian Sea and entered the Soviet airspace over Baku after four hours. Drifting for an hour, the aircraft, fitted with a 14-inch aerial camera, made six photographic runs over Baku.

Cotton flew another reconnaissance flight on 5 April again from RAF Habbaniya. This time he flew through Turkish airspace to reach Batumi in the Soviet Union. Despite encountering Soviet anti-aircraft fire and fighter interception, the flight successfully photographed the Soviet petroleum centres.

In 1946, MI6 transferred Cotton to India and based him at RAF Chaklala to oversee the Halifax overflights of RAF's No. 298 Squadron over the Soviet Union. Welsh's team also had access to Slessor for regular consultations. Cotton gained public notoriety in 1948 when he became the public face of an MI6 operation to supply arms to the Nizam of Hyderabad. This involved Cotton using a flight of six Lancaster/Lincoln aircraft to fly arms and ammunition at night from Karachi to Hyderabad. Because the Royal Indian Air Force (RIAF) then didn't have any night fighters, the aircraft couldn't be intercepted. Cotton's larger than life involvement in this operation deflected any possible attention to what he was actually doing in Pakistan.

The partition of British India and its attendant consequences were deeply entwined with and influenced by Britain's quest to develop a nuclear deterrent based on the extraction of uranium and monitoring of Soviet nuclear tests in Central Asia.

The impact on Hari Singh

Consequently, 1946 was a watershed year for Maharaja Hari Singh. His state was a composition of five parts: the Gilgit region, Ladakh, Poonch, the Kashmir Valley and Jammu. Each of them was ethnically, religiously and linguistically different from the other. In three of these parts, the Maharaja's agendas had empowered three formidable men whose actions in 1947 were not only going to dismember the state from the consolidated whole but also dispossess him and force him into exile. These men, destined to play key roles in the breaking up of the state and the unseating of the Maharaja, were Sheikh Abdullah in the Valley, Sardar Muhammad Ibrahim Khan in Poonch and Captain William Brown in the Gilgit Agency. The tragedy was that besides Abdullah, the Maharaja was completely unaware of the potential upheavals the actions of Khan and Brown could cause. Britain remained the master puppeteer pulling strings attached to these puppets one way or another.

The Maharaja's mind was so occupied with pursuing his own agendas that he had no clue of the trouble brewing right behind him. He also had no way of knowing the impact that an overt and legal departure of the British would have on his state. He had no way of knowing that Britain would covertly remain entrenched in his state and create a series of events that would ultimately exile him from his state and leave him a 'refugee royal' marking his time in isolated splendour in Bombay.

The Maharaja had forgotten that he was able to amass all this power only because the British had swung the succession pendulum in his favour. He forgot that it was only because of his father Raja Amar Singh's continued demonstrative loyalty towards the British that he got his throne. The Maharaja forgot that his predecessor, Maharaja Pratap Singh, paid a heavy price for trying to establish his independence from British control.

If the Maharaja had thought through his moves in advance and chosen to study the works of the great Indian political scientist Chanakya and followed his directives, he would never have pursued his vendetta against Raja Jagat Dev Singh of Poonch. He would have handled the British with finesse rather than imperiousness. He would have never permitted xenophobia to get out of hand and prevented the British from establishing a constitution specially tailored for his state. Chanakya's *Arthashastra* lays down the virtues of an intelligence network that informs kings and rulers not only about the plans and actions of adversaries, but also about discontent within the population.

Most importantly, he never grasped the reality that while it may have been fashionable and heady to employ British advisors and officials, their loyalty was ultimately with the British Crown.

Chapter 5

Soviet Russia Remains a Critical Threat and Opportunity

The 'new' Bose conundrum

While Stalin's closure of the Comintern in 1943 took the heat off left-sponsored agitations in India, his recognition of the Bose-led provisional Azad Hind government in November 1943 and the permission for it to open a consulate in the Soviet war-time capital of Omsk, caused a lot of unexpressed discomfort to the British. Stalin clearly intended to keep India on the back-burner only for the duration of the war.

Following Japanese Emperor Hirohito's radio broadcast on 15 August 1945 announcing Japan's intention to surrender, Bose had no option left but to flee to the Soviet Union as he was a war criminal wanted by the Allies. In one of his last messages to Nambiar, who was his 'man in Europe', he ordered the remnants of the Indian National Army (INA) in Europe, then a part of the Waffen SS, to join up with the units of the Red Army advancing towards Berlin. They were later to be deployed as the vanguard of the force that would liberate India. Bose's messages from South East Asia to Germany via the Kriegsmarine Enigma machine at the Monsun Gruppe headquarters (HQ) in Penang were intercepted by the Government Code and Cipher School at Bletchley Park in the UK. Colonel Hugh Toye of MI6 was appointed to head the outfit set up to exclusively trace and hunt down Bose.

IMAGE 5.1: Subhas Chandra Bose bidding farewell to Indian Independence League President Leon Prouchandy at the latter's Saigon residence, 18 August 1945. Source: AIM Television Archives

Bose was a master of deception. He planned his death to throw the Allies off his trail to prevent any chance of the British pressurising the Soviets to extradite him, which the Soviets were treaty-bound, to face trial for war crimes. On 17 August 1945, when Bose ostensibly took off from Saigon in a Mitsubishi 'Sally' bomber for Tourane (aka Da Nang), he was actually still in Saigon spending the night at the opulent home of Tamil-origin millionaire Leon Prouchandy, who was the President of the French Indo-China chapter of the Indian Independence League, the civilian arm of the INA. On 18 August 1945, when Bose was supposed to have been flying towards Taipei from Tourane, he was actually on another aircraft flying to Singapore. After landing in Singapore, Bose drove straight to the Japanese Southern Army HQ at Raffles College in the Bukit Timah district. From there he drove straight to Keppel Harbour where he boarded the UIT-25, a Kriegsmarine submarine flying the Japanese flag. The submarine was supposed to take Bose to the Soviet port of Vladivostok. But Bose apparently disembarked at Vladivostok on 30 August 1945 after transhipping onto a Soviet trawler just outside the Soviet territorial waters in the Sea of Japan at the spot where UIT-25 shot down a B-25 Mitchell USAAF reconnaissance aircraft. He reached Vladivostok in this trawler.

No one has bothered to ask why UIT-25 surfaced in the Sea of Japan and why the submarine engaged a low-flying American aircraft and why the submarine shot the aircraft down after all hostilities in the Pacific theatre had ceased on 15 August 1945?

UIT-25 was operating under the Japanese flag from 9 May 1945; it took the Japanese colours and a new name (I-504). The crew surrendered to the US Navy at Kobe on 2 September 1945. All the records are still classified with the US Navy. These include the logbook, the manifest and the debriefing of the surrendered crew and their nationalities. Furthermore, the complete debriefing records of Vice Admiral Paul Wenneker, the German Naval Attaché in Tokyo, also remain classified.

Therefore, it is important to reiterate that the only logical and plausible reason for UIT-25/I-504 to have surfaced in the Sea of Japan just outside Russian territorial waters was because it was transhipping its cargo and some passengers to another vessel that would carry them to Vladivostok. This transfer was highly secret, and because the USAAF aircraft presumably took photos of it, the aircraft was shot down to obliterate all evidence of the secret transfer. Presumably, Bose was part of that transhipment process.

IMAGE 5.2: Subhas Chandra Bose with INA officers, including Finance Minister Colonel A.K. Chatterjee on his left. Source: AIM Television Archives

The story has an interesting postscript. The Finance Minister of the provisional Azad Hind government, Colonel A.C. Chatterjee, and a few of his aides

flew to Hanoi on 20 August 1945 where they took shelter with the Vietminh under the command of Ho Chi Minh. Chatterjee was waiting to fly to Omsk to link up with Bose. It took quite some time, but by December 1945, it became clear that Chatterjee would be able to get an aircraft that would fly him and his men to Omsk, overflying territory controlled by Mao in the Chinese civil war. Unfortunately for Chatterjee, Ho Chi Minh betrayed him and his men to the British. MI6 officer Lieutenant Colonel A.G. Trevor-Wilson was sent to Hanoi to negotiate his arrest. Chatterjee and his party were arrested on 23 December 1945 from their safe house in Hanoi along with around one million dollars' worth of gold bars. Why was Chatterjee planning to fly to Omsk if he wasn't meeting up with Bose?

Following Chatterjee's arrest on 23 December 1945, he was flown to Singapore the next day. Two days later, on 26 December 1945, Bose made his first post-war radio broadcast to the Intelligence Bureau (IB) of India. This was followed by a second broadcast on 1 January 1946 and a third in February 1946. In the second broadcast, Bose stated that India would get freedom within two years, but not without violence. The details of the broadcasts are available in a file (No. 87011p1692 PoI) that has been declassified by the Indian government. The broadcasts were relayed on the 31-metre band. Does the same file also refer to a Cabinet meeting chaired by Prime Minister Attlee on 25 October 1945 that ostensibly discussed the options available on how to deal with Bose?

Why the Soviet-launched, Bose-led invasion plan was sidelined and modified

The jury is still out on this. Any invasion of India by land from the highlands of Soviet Central Asia through the Gilgit Agency could only be feasible if India was still under British rule, not under Dominion status, and only if the Soviet Union was willing to face the possibility of counter-attacks on Soviet assets in Sinkiang and Soviet Kazakhstan. The Soviets were in a dilemma. Allowing its territory to be used to invade India was a lesser worry for the Soviet Union as it was facing an acute existential crisis during those days. The Soviets were worried about nuclear threats from the US, against which it had no deterrence. In order to build up this deterrence, the Soviets had to accelerate the extraction of uranium ore in large quantities and also select a test site near the ore for nuclear explosions. The ore was mined in the Koktogai Valley in Kazakhstan, and aerial surveys to locate additional deposits of uranium ore were undertaken over the Altai Mountains in northern Sinkiang, the Tarim Basin, along the Karakash River in Aksai Chin and over Ili along the Soviet border. The KGB chief Lavrenti Beria solved the problem by selecting Semipalatinsk as the test site for the proposed Soviet nuclear tests. This effectively lay to waste Bose's ambitions to lead an invasion of India launched from Soviet territory. Though the Bose plan was shelved, Stalin's appetite for Sinkiang and Aksai Chin increased. Aksai Chin was ultimately invaded by his proxy.

These compulsions to develop a nuclear deterrent against the US nuclear monopoly necessitated military control over both Sinkiang and Aksai Chin and the erection of a wall of secrecy around this region as far as possible. A land invasion of India through the Pamirs or the Karakoram would have all sorts of repercussions and jeopardise Beria's well-thought-out plans. Consequently, Bose's desire to free India from British rule through an armed invasion had to wait as it didn't seem so alluring anymore. It is possible that a protest by Bose against this new Soviet stance resulted in him being sent off to the Gulag until after Stalin's death and Beria's execution.

Chitral poses a problem in connection with Bose

Chitral was the largest district in British India's NWFP. This area was the scene of Ionov's intrusions in 1891. It was separated from what was then Soviet Tajikistan by the narrow Wakhan Corridor, which extends from north-eastern Afghanistan to China. According to an IB report of 1946, Nehru received a letter from Bose stating he was in the Soviet Union and that he wanted to come to India via Chitral (File No. 223 INA). What made this letter all the more intriguing was the fact that it surfaced soon after Bose's last radio broadcast in February 1946. The icing on the cake was the presence of Burhanuddin, the Prince of Chitral, in the background to both the broadcasts and the letter.

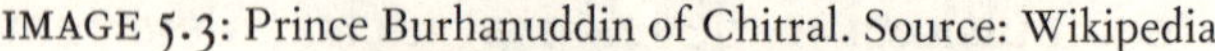

IMAGE 5.3: Prince Burhanuddin of Chitral. Source: Wikipedia

Bose's intended arrival in Chitral sent shivers down the spine of the Government of India. They did not know that Bose's 1946 plan to enter India was forcibly relegated to the back-burner by Beria. The worry in British circles was that if Prince Burhanuddin was part of the vanguard of Bose's alleged invasion force, then such a bold move could jeopardise Bacon's key nuclear monitoring empire. Burhanuddin was a key member of the INA. He was captured in Burma on 3 May 1945 and put on trial in a military court presided over by none other than the then Brigadier Kodandera Madappa Cariappa, who became the first C-in-C of the Indian Army and later on India's first Field Marshal.

It is said that after the court sentenced the prisoner to six years of rigorous imprisonment for waging war against the King-Emperor, Cariappa walked across to Burhanuddin and shook his hand. This was a move that raised many eyebrows. If this was the sentiment felt towards Burhanuddin by the senior-most serving Indian-origin officer, then how could the loyalty of the Chitral Scouts be guaranteed? The Chitral Scouts was a 1,200-strong force and the only possible defence against a Bose-led, Soviet-backed invasion of Chitral.

Bose's link with the NWFP was not, therefore, a figment of imagination of the worried officials of the Government of India. Bose himself planned attacks on British forces from the tribal areas of the NWFP. He stated in his memorandum of 9 April 1941, presented to the Nazis in Berlin soon after he arrived there, that 'our agents are already working in the independent Tribal territory lying between Afghanistan and India. Their efforts will have to be coordinated and an attack on British military centres will have to be planned on a large scale' (File No: L/P and J/12/217, Public Record Office, London). In fact, Bhagat Ram Talwar, Bose's guide in his journey from Peshawar to Kabul, also ferried revolutionaries like Sodhi Harminder Singh and Santimoy Ganguly from India in the same year for training in underground combat by Soviet GRU agents in Afghanistan. The fear was that these varied 'sleepers' would be collectively roused to undertake sabotage in advance of the Bose-led force.

What certainly happened was that any lingering doubts that some minority factions of the British establishment may have had about persuading Jinnah and Nehru to stay together after India got a Dominion status were erased forever once the Gen 75 Committee of the British Cabinet decided on the importance of Bacon's nuclear monitoring empire. It became clear that both the Gilgit Agency and the NWFP had to be sequestered from the body of India if the country was going to be led by Nehru instead of Patel. This decision had many repercussions as we shall see.

The Soviets gear up to make the atom bomb

The importance of the monitoring stations in Kashmir grew rapidly as intelligence poured in from MI6 sources in the Soviet Union, so did the need to prepare for aerial overflights above Soviet Kazakhstan, Tajikistan and Sinkiang to pick up radioactive samples to confirm the release of radiation in the atmosphere. On 9 April 1946, the Soviet Council of Ministers decided that a new laboratory called KB-11 would be created, which would be attached to Laboratory#2 at the Kurchatov Institute in Moscow. The lab would design and manufacture an actual nuclear device to be detonated at the test. KB-11 was to be located in the town of Sarov some 400 kilometres from Moscow and 75 kilometres from the city of Arzamas. The entire set-up had to be built more or less from scratch.

A new timeline was released on 21 June 1946 that specified that KB-11 had to design and manufacture the first bomb, designated RDS-1, by 1 July 1947. On 17 February 1947, KB-11 was decreed to be a top-secret establishment.

Meanwhile, the extraction of uranium ore proceeded at a feverish pace in the uranium mines of Sinkiang. The ore was mined by the Kazakhs/Uyghurs under the control of Bator. Therefore, Bator was both a labour contractor providing miners to the Soviet mines and an atomic spy for the Americans. Bator's usefulness to the Americans stemmed from the fact that he had direct access to the mines. The ore samples provided by him found their way to Gilgit through Brown's courier network. From Gilgit, they were transhipped to the UK and the US.

Parallel developments in the Valley

In snow-bound Srinagar, during the early winter months of 1946, Sheikh Abdullah began to test the waters by rocking the Maharaja's throne. In March, Abdullah instructed Beg to resign from his ministerial post. During those days, the British Cabinet Mission was in India negotiating with Jinnah and the Congress party about the mechanics for the transfer of power. There was uncertainty all around and the communal cauldron was bubbling.

In May 1946, the National Conference launched the Quit Kashmir campaign against the Maharaja. Abdullah delivered incendiary speeches and condemned the sale of the Valley to Gulab Singh by the British in 1846. He emphatically declared that this was an invalid act. It, therefore, followed that the Maharaja was an invalid ruler. He insisted that the Maharaja should leave Kashmir immediately and hand over power to the people of the state. It took 15 years of British intrigue to unleash the forces that shook the seemingly unshakeable rule of Gulab Singh's descendants.

In 1947, the kingdom of Jammu and Kashmir disintegrated. This was fuelled by political machination and intrigue throughout the previous year, which contributed to the rapid decline in the political climate of the state. To begin with, the Prime Minister of the state, Ram Chandra Kak, began to exploit the differences between Abdullah's National Conference and Shah's Muslim Conference. According to Kak, Abdullah threatened the very existence of the monarchy, therefore, he had to be defeated politically. Kak's deft political intrigue isolated the Muslim Conference from the Quit Kashmir movement. Kak placed the state under martial law and arrested almost the entire top-level leadership and hundreds of workers of the National Conference, while he spared the Muslim Conference his wrath. Abdullah was arrested and sentenced to three years imprisonment for sedition, but he escaped to Punjab, leaving the National Conference leaderless and in disarray. After some time, he clandestinely returned to Kashmir but was discovered and arrested. To outside observers like Nehru, it seemed Abdullah enjoyed popular support in the Valley since Shah appeared out of touch with the popular political sentiment. Nehru, however, failed to read the fine print. Kak also arrested Muslim Conference leader Chaudhry Ghulam Abbas to make it look fair since Abbas supported the Maharaja. This deft move politically neutralised Shah and facilitated Abbas's takeover of the Muslim Conference. An emotional Nehru decided to personally rally behind his protégé and close friend Abdullah. He first tried to persuade Kak to release Abdullah, and when this failed, he decided to pay a visit to Kak in Srinagar to try and get him to agree to his request to release Abdullah from gaol.

While crossing into Kashmir from Punjab on 21 June 1946, Nehru was detained in Uri Dak Bungalow under Kak's orders. This was a personal affront to Nehru, which made him very resentful. He resolved to bring Kak and the Maharaja down. With Viceroy Lord Archibald Percival Wavell's intervention, Nehru reached Srinagar a month later in July. He visited Abdullah in prison and attended one of his many trials. The Maharaja, however, declined to meet Nehru because he was infuriated with Nehru's clout in the British establishment that forced him to permit Nehru's entry into his state. The differences between the Maharaja and Nehru grew wider in the following years.

Nehru discounted the fact that there were four equally important constituents of Hari Singh's kingdom besides the Valley. For Nehru, the Valley was the nucleus and he imagined that it exerted a centripetal force that kept Gilgit-Baltistan, Ladakh, Muzaffarabad-Poonch and Jammu in a kind of stable orbit where Abdullah was the force of gravity. The truth was far from Nehru's interpretation. The Valley was no nucleus even though Srinagar was home to the Maharaja, the Resident and the Army chief. The other four parts of the kingdom were pulling away from the Valley with a centrifugal force that was uniquely geopolitical. The unstable orbits were held together by four men.

The first was Prime Minister Kak and his English wife Margaret. The second was Resident W.F. Webb (Indian Civil Service [ICS]). The third was the Army chief Major General H.L. Scott. And the fourth was the Inspector General (IG) of Police Richard Powell. The wives of these four men frequently played Canasta together. The families also regularly dined together. Kak was an Anglophile, but he was only a nominal brown face of an administration tightly controlled by the British. Kak's instructions from his British mentors helped prepare the ground for the state to splinter and go to Pakistan.

Kak and the British realised that Abdullah was out of their grasp. Abdullah had been promised absolute and uncontested power by Nehru. In Nehru's scheme of things, a referendum of sorts would replace the Maharaja and install Abdullah as the face of democracy. No amount of persuasion could break Abdullah from Nehru because Abdullah realised he would not be acceptable to the other constituent parts of the state as their single overlord. For Abdullah, the decoupling of the Valley from the other parts would ensure his dominance. Yet he continuously fed Nehru the fiction that he represented the popular will of all oppressed Muslims of the kingdom. Abdullah realised that he had to first depose the Maharaja and his British mentors led by Kak to get power, after which he would deal with the local competition. Nehru was Abdullah's ticket to power. For Nehru, Kashmir provided a land border with China and was contiguous with NWFP where Khan Abdul Ghaffar Khan led a Congress government. NWFP would provide India with a land border with Afghanistan. Pakistan would be a small state with only parts of Punjab, Sindh and possibly Baluchistan.

The British understood Nehru's post-Partition plan for India and worked to destroy it. Nehru's vision of India would have no place for Bacon's nuclear monitoring empire, therefore, it was imperative to shatter this vision into tiny pieces.

In his fascinating book *Unravelling the Kashmir Knot*, Aman M. Hingorani describes Viceroy of India Lord Wavell's memorandum of 30 May 1946 to the Cabinet Mission in which he argued that the Gilgit Agency part of Kashmir would necessarily have to remain within Britain's permanent sphere of influence. In Wavell's own language, that would be akin to having Northern Ireland within India.

To this end, Kak engineered Jinnah's visit to Srinagar on the basis of subtle British pressure and got him to mediate between the Muslim Conference and the National Conference in 1944 to unite the two warring factions that were working towards the same intrinsic goal. However, Jinnah was unsuccessful and ended up endorsing the Muslim Conference as the only sincere representative of the suffering Muslim masses of the state. This helped Kak introduce a nascent idea of Pakistan to the Maharaja.

But in 1946, the state's security faced newer threats. Tibet had de facto independence and was one of the countries that shared a border with Jammu and Kashmir. To secure India's borders, the British government was willing to provide military support to Tibet. In the same year, the British government officials prepared a confidential memo entitled 'Appreciation of the scale of direct military assistance which could be provided in support of Tibet'. According to this memo, Russia and China were potential threats to India's security. The memo proposed a line passing through Chamdo, Nagchuka, Garyarsa and Leh, and opined that any invasion by Russians or Chinese from south of this line would prove to be highly dangerous for India's security. The area south of this proposed line would be a buffer zone between India and the two expansionist powers Russia and China. This memo emphasised the crucial role the state of Jammu and Kashmir played in maintaining India's military defence.

IMAGE 5.4: Sir Olaf Caroe in NWFP, 1960. Source: Public Domain

Before this memo was written, India's Secretary of External Affairs Sir Olaf Caroe stated that the Gilgit-Kashgar boundary was the only direct contact point between India and China and that no other contact points should be added. Caroe was made the Governor of the NWFP in late 1946, succeeding Sir George Cunningham. Cunningham was reappointed as the Governor of the province by the new Pakistani government on 15 August 1947.

Two things are noteworthy here. First, the memo underscored the importance of Tibet as a neutral buffer zone between India and China and said it had to be defended against Chinese aggression. Second, both the NWFP and Hari Singh's kingdom of Jammu and Kashmir had to remain conjoined twins in a single political entity controlled by the British, at least till the bomb had been built and overflights above the Soviet Union were not required.

On Kak's advice endorsed by Webb, the Maharaja decided to hold elections to the state's assembly in January 1947. The allegiance of the Valley's population was divided between the National Conference and the Muslim Conference. With the National Conference boycotting the elections and the Maharaja's government keeping the remainder seats unfilled because of nomination screening, the Muslim Conference won 15 seats and secured the largest elected representation in the assembly. With this, Kak successfully crushed the slim goodwill between the National Conference and the Muslim Conference. The quarrel he engineered between Abdullah and Shah went against the original mandate of unity within the Muslim population against the Maharaja. Glancy's constitutions of 1934 and 1939 created an electoral system that, while legalising dissent and political activity, only permitted the electoral participation of 10 per cent of the population. Further, this system was vulnerable to extreme manipulation and corruption, especially in the matter of nomination. Glancy thus provided only the aroma of power to the poverty-stricken Muslim majority and instilled in them a collective desire for majority Muslim rule by rebellion against the Maharaja.

The political polarisation in the state was now complete. The National Conference allied with the Congress, and the Muslim Conference with the Muslim League. The former had almost total control in the Kashmir Valley while the latter was dominant in the Jammu province, especially in the western districts of Mirpur, Poonch and Muzaffarabad. However, both parties held ambiguous positions on the accession of the state. The National Conference demanded that the common people of Kashmir should decide on accession. The Muslim Conference was generally inclined to support accession to Pakistan, but in September 1946, it passed a resolution in favour of *azad*, or free, Kashmir. This change of stand was engineered by Kak, which allowed the Maharaja to hedge his bets till the bitter end. The Hindus, who were mostly confined to the Jammu province, were organised under Rajya Hindu Sabha led by Prem Nath Dogra. Nehru believed that Dogra was financed by the Maharaja. The Jammu Hindus mostly regarded the Maharaja as their leader and gave him total support.

Meanwhile, in Poonch, after the death of Raja Jagat Dev Singh in 1940, Maharaja Hari Singh appointed a guardian for Jagat Dev's minor son, Shiv Ratan Dev Singh, and used the opportunity to integrate the Poonch *jagir* into the state of Jammu and Kashmir. The Rajmata, Jagat Dev Singh's widow, took the young heir and fled to Nepal, fearing for their lives. Poonch became a district of Jammu administered by officers of Jammu and Kashmir. This resulted in Poonch losing its autonomy and its people being subjected to increased taxation by the Kashmir state, both of which were resented by the people. Sardar Muhammad Ibrahim Khan led the people of Poonch to protest against these measures; he was a protégé of Raja Jagat Dev Singh. Khan, who was biding his time as an agent provocateur while serving as the Assistant Advocate General of the state, resigned from his job and secured a Muslim Conference ticket to fight the assembly elections in 1947.

Both Kak and W.P. Cranson (IPS) were delighted that a non-Valley, British-educated Muslim, who ostensibly shared their strategic vision, would be a member of the legislative assembly and amenable to manipulation by them. Little did Kak and Cranson know that the seeds of revenge and rebellion had already been planted in Sardar Muhammad Ibrahim Khan's mind by Raja Jagat Dev Singh. Khan won the election from the Bagh Sudhanoti constituency. The time was ripe to seek vengeance and a motive presented itself. By his own account, Khan was thoroughly convinced that a conspiracy was being planned jointly by state forces and the RSS, so he mobilised the people of Poonch politically and set in motion a chain of events that led to the formation of Azad Kashmir some months later.

Chapter 6

Mountbatten's Unseemly Moves

A crumbling empire

The empire was beginning to crumble. Predictably, it started to happen in India. In an unprecedented move, the RAF mutinied in 1946. There were a series of demonstrations and strikes at several dozen RAF stations in India and South East Asia in January 1946. The protests arose from slow demobilisation and poor conditions of service following the end of the Second World War. The mutiny began at the RAF's Drigh Road station in Karachi. It later spread to involve nearly 50,000 men over 60 RAF stations in India and Ceylon. It also enveloped the then-largest RAF base at Cawnpore, now Kanpur, and far-off RAF bases such as in Singapore.

This contagion set a precedent and instigated future mutinies, first by members of the Indian Air Force (IAF) and then the Navy. In February 1946, 78 out of 88 ships mutinied in Bombay and Karachi. Lord Wavell, the Viceroy of India at that time, conceded that both the mutinies considerably undermined the power of British authority in India. The Indian Army POWs revolted in Germany in 1941 and Singapore in 1942 and consolidated to form the INA under the leadership of Subhas Chandra Bose. The INA fought the British Army not only in Western Europe but also in Burma and North-Eastern India. It lost in every theatre it fought. However, an irreparable trust deficit had been created and the British could no longer trust the officers of the Indian Army to sustain and preserve British rule in India. Further, IB intercepts of radio broadcasts ostensibly sent by Bose in December 1945 and January 1946 struck fear in British intelligence circles and made them fear the consequences of Bose's army attacking them from the USSR.

Amid all this turmoil, Attlee's Cabinet decided in February 1947 to wind down all British overseas commitments that would prove difficult to sustain in the future. However, British shipping through Suez had to be protected along with the bases in Aden, Hong Kong and Singapore. There was a growing communist insurgency in both Malaysia and Indonesia, and India's Congress party was objecting to the use of Indian troops to fight in these countries as well as in the Middle East. The emerging Cold War in Europe entailed the diversion of resources to protect Western Europe and to develop a British nuclear deterrence. Something had to give way. Weighed against all these responsibilities, India, the jewel in the crown of the British Empire, would have to be abandoned.

This panoply of events on the world stage proved to be too much of a burden for Attlee's government, and they decided to find a candidate for the Viceroy of India, someone who would replace Wavell and handle the winding up of the British Raj in India in such a manner that vital British interests like the protection and preservation of Bacon's nuclear monitoring empire was adequately secured. Attlee had to find an appropriate person on the ground who was endowed with considerable authority. He offered the job to the person he thought would best fit the bill for this job.

This person was King George VI's cousin, Lord Louis Mountbatten. No historian has provided a plausible reason for this appointment. Mountbatten always dreamed of serving as First Sea Lord of the Royal Navy, a post he took charge of in 1955 and held for four years. In Britain's naval history, Mountbatten and his father were the only father-son duo to have ever served in this post. Mountbatten also served as UK's Chief of Defence Staff. He was the longest-serving professional military officer in the British Armed Forces. He retired in 1965. No historian has examined whether Churchill, Ismay and Cunningham influenced Attlee in his decision to appoint Mountbatten as the last Viceroy of India.

IMAGE 6.1: Prime Minister Winston Churchill (sitting) with (L–R) Lord Ismay and Lord Mountbatten. Source: Wikimedia Commons

Mountbatten was a member of the British royal family and a former commander of British forces in South East Asia. Could this complex task have been entrusted to a safer pair of hands? Was there anyone safer than a member of the British royal family and a distinguished military man to handle this delicate task? Did Churchill brief Mountbatten before the latter accepted the job? Was Lord Ismay's appointment as Mountbatten's Chief of Staff Churchill's idea? Was Ismay's appointment Churchill's way of making sure that Mountbatten toed the Churchillian line to the hilt?

Declassified secret records can never be trusted to reveal the true import of the recorded events. Countless decisions and orders issued as a consequence of decisions taken in the British system are verbal, particularly where national security is concerned. Some records are never released, like the records of Mountbatten's communications to London as Governor-General of India after the transfer of power. They are still classified 75-long years later.

Mountbatten opens his account

Mountbatten's appointment was preceded by a meeting of the British Gen 163 Cabinet committee on 8 January 1947.

Nearly a year earlier on 25 December 1946, Kurchatov's reactor F-1 started producing a nuclear reaction. MI6 obtained a vital piece of intelligence from a secure source in the Kremlin that Stalin was set to meet Soviet's nuclear czar Igor Kurchatov on 9 January 1947.

IMAGE 6.2: Father of Soviet H-Bomb Andrei Sakharov (left) and Father of Soviet A-Bomb Igor Kurchatov. Source: Wikipedia

Also invited were Khariton, Kikoin and Artsimovich, who were the scientific leaders of the atomic cities. Also attending were Molotov, Beria, Malenkov, Voznesensky and Pervukhin. Special Committee members—Vannikov, Zavenyagin and Makhneyev—were also invited. NKVD Major General A.H. Komarovsky, head of Glavpromstroy PGY, atomic gulag, was also present in the list. None of those participating in the meeting left any kind of note of the meeting. The regime of secrecy prohibited making such notes. This was to date the most important meeting ever held in the Soviet Union to discuss nuclear issues. While authentic information on the proceedings would not be easily available, what was clear was that the Soviets were racing ahead with their first nuclear test in Semipalatinsk.

Further, Combine6 located in Khojand, Tajikistan, was the key unit producing uranium blocks out of uranium ore. NKVD Colonel B.N. Chirkov was appointed as the Combine's first director. Both

Semipalatinsk and Khojand became vital targets for aerial reconnaissance by the British. The Joint Air Photographic Intelligence Board (UK) in liaison with TAL determined the frequency and number of targets to be covered by aerial reconnaissance sorties flown out of RAF Chaklala and RAF Risalpur. These were all black operation flights.

In addition, the Abbottabad Signals Intelligence (SIGNIT) station of the Indian Army was directed to solely focus on SIGINT traffic out of the southern Soviet Union and Sinkiang. The focus was on Kashgar, Urumqi, Semipalatinsk and Khojand.

Professor H.I.S. Thirlway, an eminent British seismologist, was under consideration to head the seismic monitoring station Stowage. He reported directly to Welsh in London. Clearly, Bacon's nuclear monitoring empire was Britain's most vital resource in enabling it to claw into the nuclear club.

The British could not afford to be left behind and needed to know what the Soviet nuclear scientists were going to be doing over the next few years. The new Viceroy would have to perform the delicate task of 'officially' winding down Britain's role in India while physically retaining secure control of the Gilgit Agency-based monitoring and study of Soviet nuclear tests in Semipalatinsk.

Mountbatten arrived in India to take over as the Viceroy on 22 March 1947. By this time, the Government of India had a clear idea as to what Maharaja Hari Singh intended to do after the transfer of power in June 1948. If possible he would prefer to opt for a quasi-independent status with Pakistan. He already had bad blood with Nehru, and Abdullah continued to be a thorn in his side. The Maharaja needed to free himself from slow strangulation if political reform was forced on Kashmir after denying him quasi-independence. Kak had his eyes set on striking a deal with the emerging state of Pakistan. In his dispatch from Srinagar on 14 November 1946, the British Resident in Jammu and Kashmir, Webb, reported as much to Viceroy Wavell.

It had been a major objective of British policy from the 19th century to insulate the state of Jammu and Kashmir from Russian influence. After the start of the Cold War, the possibility of Subhas Chandra Bose's refuge in the Soviet Union, the Soviet presence in Sinkiang and the selection of Semipalatinsk as the site of proposed Soviet nuclear tests posed potential threats to the security of Jammu and Kashmir, thereby threatening the stability of the post-independent government in the state. All of these interests would be best served if Jammu and Kashmir had been prevented from being the site of further foreign policy experiments. Resolute control over the state was clearly called for and many in the British administration believed that a Pakistan under British supervision was better equipped to exercise this control than India.

On 29 April 1947, Mountbatten took a calculated decision and displayed his awareness of the undercurrents and complications of the Gilgit lease when he advised Lord Listowel, Secretary of State for India in the British government, on the future of the lease. At this point, the date for the transfer of power was still known to be 30 June 1948. Mountbatten recommended that the entire area of Gilgit be returned to the state of Jammu and Kashmir well before June 1948 and as early as October 1947. Listowel agreed and Nehru, too, concurred when consulted. Jinnah, for the record, was not asked for his opinion.

In the backdrop of what was happening in Sinkiang, it became difficult to make a case for transferring the responsibility of defending Gilgit to Maharaja Hari Singh. It was largely to keep the area out of Hari Singh's hands that the Gilgit lease was secured in the first place. Yet, here was Mountbatten apparently abandoning this vital outpost and handing it back to Hari Singh. This was a paradox, which only made sense on the assumption that the new lessees of the Gilgit lease would be based not in Srinagar and Jammu but Karachi.

Why did Mountbatten take this new decision? Did Attlee tell him to rescind the Gilgit lease to enable a quiet and legal transfer of Kashmir to Pakistan?

It is being argued here that Mountbatten was issued top-secret instructions in London before he left for India to take up the post of Viceroy. As mentioned earlier, Mountbatten's overriding orders from the British government were to secure the 'cast-iron' safety and continued existence of the three British nuclear monitoring stations in Gilgit, notwithstanding the transfer of power. This was the decision of the Gen 163 Cabinet committee that succeeded the Gen 75 Committee in January 1947. Since the balance was tilted in favour of Maharaja Hari Singh's accession to Pakistan, it became imperative to ensure that the entire kingdom, including the Gilgit Agency, passed peacefully into Pakistan's willing hands. This would also provide complementary support to the British plan of including NWFP in Pakistan so that the entire range of British India's north-western borders would devolve into Pakistan.

The author Aman Hingorani refers to Mountbatten's interview with the authors Larry Collins and Dominique Lapierre, who wrote the famous book *Freedom at Midnight*. In this interview, Mountbatten said he wanted Kashmir to accede to Pakistan simply because it made Pakistan all the more viable. Since he was responsible for the creation of Pakistan, he wanted it to work, he said, and it would work better with Kashmir. By achieving this, his creation had a better chance of surviving.

What Mountbatten was presumably loath to admit or reveal to Collins and Lapierre was that Britain's quest to join the nuclear club made it imperative that both the Gilgit Agency and the Muzaffarabad-Poonch belt remained under British physical influence and official Pakistani control. With both of these in the bag, if it was possible to also add the Valley, then that would be a bonus.

Mountbatten arrived in London in the middle of May in 1947. The issue of the NWFP was critical to the existence of Bacon's nuclear monitoring empire because Risalpur airfield was needed for certain overflights above the Soviet Union. Also, the joker in the pack was the role of all the Pathan Scouts and levies raised since 1946.

The date for transfer of power is suddenly brought forward

On or around 31 May 1947, Major General Stewart Menzies (also C and head of MI6), drove from MI6

HQ at 54 Broadway to 10 Downing Street. He had an urgent appointment with Prime Minister Attlee. On the cards was a top-secret 'for your eyes only' briefing on the latest intelligence about the Soviet nuclear programme. Top secret MI6-controlled RAF reconnaissance flights from Chaklala outside Rawalpindi over the selected Soviet test site of Semipalatinsk revealed activities involving the construction of buildings, railway lines and an airfield. Intelligence from Moscow revealed that the Kurchatov Institute, which was designing the first Soviet nuclear weapon at the site called KB-11, had made key breakthroughs, leading to the start of prototype construction of the weapon. The construction of the Mayak plutonium plant in the southern Urals was being driven at a scorching pace by Beria. Combine6 at Khojand was also working round the clock to produce uranium blocks. It was imperative to put in place all the cogs in Bacon's nuclear monitoring empire.

To C's surprise, Mountbatten was also present at this meeting. All three of them agreed that Bacon's entire set-up had to be made secure. For that to happen, both NWFP and Kashmir had to remain under secure British control for as long as required, notwithstanding independence and partition. Mountbatten left for India shortly after this meeting.

All the records of C's meetings with Attlee and what transpired during these meetings would not be recorded, particularly if deemed to be highly sensitive and at variance with the government's official position, or those matters that, in the public domain, could appear to be unprincipled. It is my assessment that given the pattern of events, this meeting had to have happened.

On 4 June 1947, immediately after his return from London, Mountbatten announced 15 August 1947 as the deadline for the transfer of power, instead of sticking to the earlier target date of 30 June 1948. Did Mountbatten spring this surprise as a result of his meeting with both C and Attlee a few days earlier?

Mountbatten had to urgently decide the future of the NWFP. This was to be brought about by a referendum with a clear choice for the voters to choose between India and Pakistan. The two Khan brothers, Abdul Ghaffar Khan aka 'Frontier Gandhi' and Dr Khan Sahib, were Congressmen and the ruling dominant political force in NWFP. They wanted the removal of Sir Olaf Caroe from his post of the Governor of NWFP. Nehru ensured that Mountbatten got his deal, provided Caroe was removed. Mountbatten got his deal through. For the British, ultimately replacing Caroe with Cunningham was going to be a good deal for what Cunningham could achieve was not possible through Caroe.

General Sir Robert Lockhart was appointed as the new Governor to oversee the referendum in NWFP in July 1947. The Congress officially boycotted the referendum. Despite this, only 50.49 per cent voted for Pakistan.

For Mountbatten, the complex problem of the future of Jammu and Kashmir and Hyderabad remained, both of which indicated an interest in being independent states after Partition. Mountbatten made it abundantly clear that he was personally unhappy about the prospect of independence for either. Given the 'historical unreliability' of Maharaja Hari Singh, both Mountbatten and Ismay were convinced that an 'independent' Jammu and Kashmir could not be relied upon to permit the British monitoring stations to remain in existence. On 9 June 1947, he announced that he was instructing the British Residents in both states to urge the rulers to make no announcements about independence until he had had the opportunity to visit them and discuss the matter.

What does become clear is that Mountbatten's changing the date of the transfer of power and bringing it forward by ten and a half months completely obscured, from the minds of both the Congress and Muslim League, thoughts about the wider geopolitical consequences of splitting Punjab in two. The approaching reality of Pakistan became a novel idea that was so overwhelming and daunting that it drowned all else including thoughts about the future of Kashmir. Further, the draft of the Indian Independence Act, by which power was to be transferred, had a joker in the pack, and that was the handing back of paramountcy in princely India to the princes. They would decide whether to join India or Pakistan or remain independent. In the rush to the new date of 15 August 1947 for the transfer of power, no direct thought was given to what was really happening in Kashmir and what the British were really up to. Mountbatten had, as far as possible, isolated Kashmir from the focus of immediate attention, which was the forthcoming partition of both Punjab and Bengal.

IMAGE 6.3: (L–R) Lord Mountbatten, Mohammed Ali Jinnah and Edwina Mountbatten. Source: Wikipedia

Mountbatten, accompanied by Lady Mountbatten and Lord Ismay, arrived in Srinagar on 17 June 1947 and was back in New Delhi six days later. During these crucial six days, he aimed to engage in detailed parleys with Hari Singh and Kak. Mountbatten asked Nehru to prepare an exhaustive briefing note on Kashmir for him, which would provide him with talking points for the ensuing discussions. While in Srinagar, Mountbatten was frustrated because Hari Singh was unwilling to engage in any serious discussions with him. The Maharaja had picked up gossip about Nehru's friendship with Edwina Mountbatten and his extraordinary closeness to the couple while Jinnah was kept at arm's length by the Mountbatten's. To Hari Singh, Lord Mountbatten was merely a votary of Nehru's views on the future of the state. He did not allow Mountbatten to visit Sheikh Abdullah in prison, even with Nehru's intervention. Lady Mountbatten found it impracticable to meet Begum Abdullah, and Mountbatten did not attempt to visit Chaudhry Ghulam Abbas and other political prisoners close to the Maharaja or to seek the views of the Mirwaiz.

The internal politics of the Valley was of no interest to Mountbatten because he knew it would be going to Pakistan lock, stock and barrel. He did, however, engage with Kak. What transpired in their conversation was not recorded. What they said in public or to the press later was an obfuscation of reality.

Both Mountbatten and Ismay were in sync on this one. They ensured in tandem that no one could guess their hidden agenda. Did this action of Mountbatten propel Ismay to sound out Bacon to also start planning for the execution of the Gilgit rebellion as a fallback plan?

Messervy makes his moves

On 23 July 1947, the General Officer Commanding (GOC) of the Northern Command of the consolidated Indian Army, Lieutenant General Sir Frank Messervy, issued orders for reconstitution of his command. This plan involved the removal of 14 battalions deployed on frontier defence. Four battalions of the Zhob Brigade were also withdrawn and tribal levies took their place. Three battalions from the Tal Brigade were removed and replaced by Frontier Scouts and *khassadars*. Four battalions from the Gardal Brigade were to be withdrawn in two phases: on 15 August and 1 October 1947. One battalion stationed at Malakand was removed earlier in July 1947. The Wana and Kohat Brigades were also reduced in size. The decision of the gradual withdrawal of Indian Army troops from the frontier was made by Field Marshal Auchinleck long before the Partition of India, and the process was already underway at the time of Partition.

Ismay mandates Bacon

What did 'Pug' Ismay do during Mountbatten's visit to Srinagar? Ismay, fluent in both Urdu and Punjabi, is reported to have conferred with the Maharaja in Punjabi and with Kak in Urdu. His conversations are not a part of the official record. What did he discuss with Kak and the Maharaja? Ismay was a discreet member of the British establishment and carried all of his secrets to his grave. He never left any papers or diaries. We can safely infer that not only did Ismay meet Bacon in Srinagar, but he also met Major General Scott, Chief of Staff of the Jammu and Kashmir state forces. It is obvious that the issue of the state forces manning the Gilgit Agency would have come up in these conversations since the lease was likely to be rescinded before the transfer of power on 15 August 1947. In that event, who would be the Political Agent? Would the Gilgit Scouts accept a non-British officer? Maybe they would accept a Muslim officer? But they would certainly not accept a Hindu officer. From where would Scott source such an officer? Bacon would move to Peshawar as Political Agent, running his 'nuclear monitoring empire' from there, and report directly to Commander Eric Walsh at TAL in London. This was in preparation for eventually bringing the Gilgit Agency under the administrative control of the Governor of NWFP if required.

Confident that all loose ends were now tied up, on his return to Delhi, Mountbatten announced that the Gilgit lease would be rescinded on 31 July 1947. On orders from Welsh in London, Bacon immediately summoned Brown who was then stationed in Waziristan as Major with the Tochi Scouts. In Waziristan, Brown had sounded out Captain Jock Mathieson and primed him to become his deputy in Gilgit if and when the eventuality arose. During the first week of July 1947, Brown met Bacon. Bacon had already passed on Welsh's orders for Scott to convince the Maharaja to appoint British officers as Commandant and Deputy Commandant of the Gilgit Scouts until a more 'suitable' arrangement was made. Both of these officers would report to the Kashmir state-appointed Political Agent or Governor. The names of the officers selected for the jobs were Brown and Mathieson.

This arrangement had a hidden subtext. Both these British officers would have to resign their respective commissions with the British Army. What was the need for this, unless Bacon had some questionable tasks in mind for these officers when he spoke with Brown? What were these questionable tasks and what were the assurances and incentives offered to these young men to quit their coveted commissions? Bacon wanted these young men to operate at an arm's length from the British government in their private capacities as mercenaries. Ismay was worried about the possibility of diplomatic flak—if it ever came out that serving British officers had participated in a conspiracy to execute the Gilgit Rebellion, the objectives of the British Parliament would be defeated and there would be a monumental scandal. Ismay was only too aware of the impact of the 1946 RAF mutiny.

It is obvious that Whitehall wanted the preservation of the Gilgit Agency under Pax Britannica, and the method by which this could be effected, despite Partition, would be to make the Gilgit Agency an agency of the NWFP, directly under its Governor. On Partition, Cunningham was to take over as the Governor of NWFP. The preparations would then be complete.

Having obtained Brown's and Mathieson's consent, Bacon flew back to Srinagar the very next day to swing these appointments. Indirect endorsement of their acceptance came in the form of an urgent wireless message from the IG of the Frontier Corps; Brown was asked to reach the Bala Hisar Fort, Peshawar. At the fort, the IG presented a way out for Brown if he wished to reconsider this assignment. Brown, however, stuck to his mission. On 29 July 1947, Brown boarded a Harvard trainer aircraft and flew to Gilgit. That this was possible so fast reveals that the conspiracy to execute the Gilgit Rebellion was thought-out well in advance, had key British players and was intended to defeat any attempt by the Maharaja to accede to India on or around 15 August 1947.

The following day, the Raja of Puniyal, the Governor of Koh-e-Khizr, one Ishkoman from the Khuswaqt family of Chitral and Raja Mehboob of Yasin had a series of closed-door meetings with Bacon and Brown. All of these men were made privy to the events that were going to unfold if Hari Singh acceded to India. While this conspiracy was being put in place, what were Mountbatten and Nehru doing? Mountbatten was circumspect, so he undoubtedly misled Nehru by guardedly discussing with him his apprehensions about Srinagar and the layers of intrigue shrouding it, and used these to deflect Nehru from ever finding out the true story. There is enough evidence to suggest that Mountbatten shared his apprehensions with Nehru and Sardar Patel and alerted them to the fact that he sensed some trouble brewing in Gilgit. The three men persuaded Mahatma Gandhi into meeting the Maharaja in Srinagar as a final effort to persuade the Maharaja to accede to India. All this was done to ensure that the Maharaja does not opt for independence.

Hari Singh gets back Gilgit

A day after the Gilgit lease was rescinded, two significant events happened in Jammu and Kashmir on 1 August 1947. Up in the north in Gilgit, an Avro Anson aircraft landed at 10:00 AM. The first to disembark was Scott, followed by Governor-designate Brigadier Ghansara Singh and Captain M. Said of the Jammu and Kashmir state forces. The next day, the ceremonial handover was completed. Scott, Bacon and Brown reportedly fine-tuned the options for the Gilgit Rebellion as news came through of Gandhi's arrival in Srinagar the previous day. Gandhi arrived in Srinagar on 1 August 1947 by road via Rawalpindi. According to A.M. Watali, who witnessed the scene as a teenager (he retired in 1987 as the IG of the Valley), Gandhi arrived in a convertible whose hood was drawn down. Thousands of people had collected in what is now the Batamaloo bus stand, and the crowd continued up to where the Badshah Bridge now stands. From the bus stand till the Old Secretariat and right up to the Maharaja's palace on Gupkar Road, there was a sea of people. They were only shouting one slogan: '*Baghi Abdullah ki jai*' (All hail to Abdullah). Watali saw Gandhi covering his ears because the reverberations of this continuous chant were too uncomfortable to bear. It was a spontaneous upsurge of popular support for Abdullah. A visibly moved Gandhi experienced personally the kind of popular support that Abdullah enjoyed in the Valley. But was Gandhi aware that this volume of public support for Abdullah was only restricted to the Valley?

With great difficulty, the driver of Gandhi's car drove him to the house of Seth Kishorilal in the Barzulla suburb of Srinagar, where he was to stay. Later in the evening around 5:00 PM, Gandhi drove up to the palace and met the Maharaja and the Maharani. He appeared to have convinced the Maharaja to release Abdullah from prison, remove Kak from his position and swiftly make up his mind about accession. As dusk descended, the palace and the city were celebrating the return of the Gilgit Agency to the rule of the Maharaja. Gandhi, it appeared, frowned on this celebration and curiously observed and prophesied that the Gilgit Agency would ultimately be snatched away. Gandhi's curious observations only underscored his knowledge, albeit limited, of what was brewing in the highlands.

Hari Singh turned a deaf ear to Gandhi's foreboding on the Gilgit Agency, finding false comfort in Scott, Kak and Ghansara Singh's assurances. Hari Singh never granted any of Gandhi's wishes and never issued orders to release Abdullah from prison. Nehru and Mountbatten felt that the Maharaja was apprehensive because Kashmir would have no land link with the prospective Indian Territory post the transfer of power. What could Nehru and Mountbatten do to reassure the nervous Maharaja? To be sure, all land routes connecting Kashmir to the Indian mainland passed through undivided Punjab, and the fear was that this part of Punjab would go to Pakistan after Partition. However, if the three eastern tehsils of the Gurdaspur district were to be awarded to India by the Punjab Boundary Commission, the accession of Jammu and Kashmir to India would be possible, provided the Maharaja cast his lot with India.

Chapter 7

Deception and Intrigue as the Transfer of Power Takes Place

The plot thickens

On 8 August 1947, a provisional map was released by the Punjab Boundary Commission that showed three eastern tehsils of Gurdaspur district falling under India even though they had slim Muslim majorities. On 12 August, when the final report of the boundary commission was released, India was not only rewarded with the three eastern tehsils of Gurdaspur but also one tehsil from Ferozepur and another from Zira on grounds of accessibility to good irrigation.

Mountbatten was suspected to have intervened in this award. The author Alastair Lamb alludes to the fact that Mountbatten was suspected to have called up Punjab Governor Sir Ewan Jenkins on 10 August. Mountbatten apparently ordered Jenkins to nudge Sir Cyril Radcliffe, who headed the Radcliffe Boundary Commission for Punjab, to award the five aforementioned tehsils to India. Why did Mountbatten provide India with a road link to Kashmir, which in turn ostensibly gave Hari Singh a chance to keep his options for merger open beyond 15 August?

IMAGE 7.1: Jawaharlal Nehru (left) and Mohammed Ali Jinnah in Simla, 1946. Source: Wikipedia

While the jury is still out on this, it appears that Mountbatten wanted to deflect Nehru's attention away from rumours in Punjab about Poonch and Gilgit, and also impress upon Nehru that he was siding with India on Kashmir. This could be the only plausible reason because the messages sent to New Delhi by Cranson pointed to intense confabulations the Maharaja was having with his wife and her brother, Nishchant Chand Katoch. Both of them wanted Kak sacked and the state merged with India. The IB bugged Hari Singh's palace and recorded all his conversations.

The Maharaja took the first tangible step towards accession to India on 11 August when he sacked

Prime Minister Kak. After his sacking, Kak was arrested at Srinagar airport while boarding an aircraft with his English wife Margaret. It is said that both Richard Powell, IG of Police, and Scott assisted him in this foiled attempt at escape. The enraged Maharaja placed him under house arrest. So, by 12 August 1947, the Maharaja had travelled one-third of the way to fulfilling Gandhi's wishes.

The sacking of Kak threw a spanner in the works. Cranson was almost certain that Hari Singh would not opt for a merger with Pakistan. Did Mountbatten's gambit backfire or was there a backup plan in the offing?

Meanwhile, Kak's ouster had other consequences. The cadres of the Muslim Conference were getting very restive, particularly after Kak's sacking. There were demonstrations in Srinagar every day. In the midst of all this, the Maharaja installed Major General Janak Singh as the new Prime Minister on 12 August 1947.

The Maharaja also relied on a trusted coterie of friends whom he used as a sounding board. This included Ram Lal Batra, who was made Deputy Prime Minister; Swami Sant Dev, who became the Maharaja's spiritual advisor and the Maharaja's close friend Victor Rosenthal. These people were clearly inadequate for the task they were picked. How would Jammu and Kashmir survive as an independent entity from 15 August 1947? The team of Janak Singh and Batra neither had the kind of relationship with Scott and Powell that Kak enjoyed nor the skill of Kak. The mere fact that both these British officers assisted Kak in his aborted escape from

Srinagar confirms their admiration and respect for Kak, which the Janak Singh-Batra duo was unlikely to enjoy. This became apparent on 12 August 1947 from their handling of the ground reality. Both Janak Singh and Batra were relatively ineffective in dealing with law and order and external security. In fact, after the removal of Kak, and given the obvious mistrust of Scott and Powell, it became clear that the new, weakened political leadership of the state was ripe for exploitation.

The Mir of Hunza makes an overture to the Chinese

There were other developments as well. In the summer of 1947, sensing the inevitability of partition, the Mir of Hunza Mohammad Jamal Khan dispatched a two-man mission to Kashgar to explore the resumption of ties with the Chinese Nationalist Party or KMT government that controlled Sinkiang. He wanted to keep his post-partition options open. The Mir, who was already a vassal ruler of the state of Jammu and Kashmir, also paid a visit to Maharaja Hari Singh in Srinagar. In his meeting with the Maharaja, the Mir of Hunza learned that the Maharaja had retracted from his earlier policy of merger with Pakistan. While the Mir was in Srinagar, the Chinese Deputy C-in-C of the Sinkiang Garrison Force in southern Sinkiang, General Zhao Xiguang, decided to personally visit Hunza to examine the opportunity that was emerging.

When the Indian Consulate in Kashgar came to know of these developments, Limbuwala, the Parsee radio operator at the Consulate sent a wireless message to Brown in Gilgit. Brown passed this news up the chain of command and was ordered to dispatch a force of Gilgit Scouts who intercepted Zhao's party and forced them to turn back. Zhao's move was interpreted by Welsh at TAL in London as being orchestrated by the Soviets. Like the Chitral scare the previous year, a new threat placed Bacon's nuclear monitoring empire once again in the arc of insecurity. Clearly, both the Gilgit Agency and the Valley had to be properly secured. Nothing short of military action would suffice. The entire region must be put under de facto British control at the very least.

Mountbatten realised this could never happen if he was a Joint Governor-General of the two emerging Dominions of India and Pakistan. Cunningham was instructed to inform Jinnah that there would now be no last-minute stepping down by him in favour of Mountbatten as Governor-General of Pakistan. Mountbatten's vain dream was sacrificed at the altar of necessity. He would now be the head of the aggrieved party when the invasion happened and secure a peace that would protect British interests.

The standstill agreements

During his June visit to Jammu and Kashmir, Mountbatten suggested that the state secure standstill agreements with both India and Pakistan. Such agreements would enable the state to continue to enjoy trade, communication and service arrangements it had enjoyed within British India. On 12 August

1947, after taking charge as Prime Minister, the first thing Janak Singh had to do was to send telegrams to both the emerging Dominions of India and Pakistan, proposing parallel standstill agreements. The telegram sent to the Government of India stated that Jammu and Kashmir would welcome a standstill agreement with the Union of India on all matters that existed between the state and the outgoing British India government. It suggested that the existing arrangements should continue until the formal execution of fresh arrangements. These arrangements, according to the Treaty of Amritsar of 1846, mandated the use of Indian forces in the event of internal rebellion or invasion by a foreign power.

On 15 August 1947, Pakistan agreed to sign a standstill agreement with Jammu and Kashmir. Under this agreement, the Pakistani government assumed charge of the postal and telegraph systems of Jammu and Kashmir and agreed to supply foodstuffs and other essential commodities to the state. However, the Government of India demurred. Could the Indian government help Jammu and Kashmir, without recourse to the proposed standstill agreement or/and the Instrument of Accession, if the state was besieged by internal rebellion or external invasion? Did Mountbatten cancel the Gilgit lease so that it would not even have an iota of contingent residual validity if the proposed standstill agreement was not signed with India?

There was deception and intrigue at every corner. There were traps and fallback positions at every stage. It appears that the entire exercise was manipulated to ensure that Bacon's nuclear monitoring empire was protected.

Someone at the highest level in the Government of India stalled the signing of the standstill agreement to buy time for a military intervention in Jammu and Kashmir to secure British interests.

Cunningham takes charge in NWFP

Sir George Cunningham was sworn in as the third-time Governor of NWFP on 15 August 1947. He was placed there by Ismay and Auchinleck for a purpose—he could successfully motivate frontier tribesmen to invade Kashmir. In the period just before the transfer of power, almost every tribe on the frontier was asking him to let them go so that they could go ahead and kill Sikhs. Pleased with his hold over the tribes of NWFP, Cunningham wrote, 'I would only have to hold up my little finger to get a *lashkar* of 40,000 or 50,000.' Cunningham found that internal tribal dynamics and local political manoeuvring determined who went to Kashmir. NWFP Chief Minister-designate Khan Abdul Qayyum Khan and Muslim League supporter Pir of Manki Sharif lobbied Pashtuns for the Kashmir invasion. These were Pashtuns from Mardan and Swat. Some were Pashto and Hindko speakers; others were Mahsud, Afridi, Mohmand and Bajaur tribesmen. It was quite a motley crew. Abdul Qayyum Khan and the Pir of Manki Sharif were the two recruiting agents deployed by Cunningham to raise his ragtag army of tribesmen that would, in the years to come, lay the grounds for sustained and never-ending militancy in Jammu and Kashmir.

Mountbatten takes over de facto political and executive control

In the interview with Collins and Lapierre, Mountbatten said he was sounded out by both Patel and Nehru to take on a more active role in governing post-partition India. This culminated in the creation of an Emergency Committee in the Indian Cabinet chaired by Mountbatten, with Nehru on his right and Patel on his left. For the record, Mountbatten would consult both Patel and Nehru separately but propose decisions unquestioningly endorsed by both. In his monumental work *The Great Divide: Britain–India–Pakistan*, H.V. Hodson reveals that Mountbatten took a number of key decisions as Chairman of the Emergency Committee of the Union Cabinet. One of which was to set up a Defence Committee of the Cabinet. The Cabinet then invited him to also become the Chairman of the Defence Committee. Mountbatten readily agreed to this. Events enabled Mountbatten to inveigle himself into dominating the post Partition government of the Dominion of India and thereby unhesitatingly defend British interests. Mountbatten thus became the most effective insurance policy to prevent no-holds-barred war between India and Pakistan, so that Bacon's nuclear monitoring empire would not experience any collateral damage as a consequence of such a war.

General Lockhart stumbles

IMAGE 7.2: General Rob Lockhart. Source: Wikipedia

According to a biography of Major General A.A. 'Jick' Rudra, who was the Military Secretary to General Lockhart after the latter took over as the C-in-C of the Indian Army on 15 August 1947, both Lockhart and General Gracey of the Pakistan Army spoke daily on the phone, particularly so after *kabailis* (raiders) began congregating in the Attock-Rawalpindi area in the second half of October 1947. By then the invasion of Poonch was also about to begin. Gracey would give a fairly detailed assessment about everything to Lockhart on a day-to-day basis. So, it would not be far from the truth to assert that Lockhart had advanced information on the strength of the *kabaili* force and its intentions. He, however, kept this information from the general staff, his political boss Defence Minister Sardar Baldev Singh as well as Prime Minister Nehru.

There are no records of the potentially explosive Gracey-Lockhart conversations. There are also no records or evidence of whether or not and with what frequency Lockhart spoke to the Governor of NWFP Sir George Cunningham, his successor, and how deep, if at all, Lockhart was involved with these two individuals in what can easily be called a 'conspiracy of silence'. Another possible member of this conspiracy, if it existed, was Sir Francis Mudie, Governor of West Punjab from 15 August 1947 to 2 August 1949.

IMAGE 7.3: General Douglas Gracey. Source: Wikipedia

Mudie, Governor of West Punjab, and Cunningham, Governor of NWFP, were both British. It can be argued that both West Punjab and NWFP were integral to the security of both British nuclear monitoring stations and the overflights above the Soviet Union from RAF Chaklala near Rawalpindi and RAF Risalpur in NWFP. Therefore, unlike Sindh which was not important from the British point of view and which had a Pakistani Governor S.G.H. Hidayatullah, both Punjab and NWFP could not be entrusted to Pakistanis and were, therefore, governed by British civil servants of the ICS.

IMAGE 7.4: Nuclear scientist Albert Einstein with Prime Minister Nehru at Princeton, New Jersey, 1949. Source: Wikipedia

In December 1947 when the fighting in Kashmir began to take a turn for the worse, Nehru was tipped off about Lockhart's 'silence'. Apparently, Nehru confronted Lockhart about this fact, to which the latter confessed that in the circumstances he may have been remiss in his duties. Nehru apparently then turned to him and asked him if his general sympathies were with Pakistan. Lockhart is said to have replied that since Nehru had to ask him that question, there was clearly a lack of trust, so he offered to resign. Lockhart was shamed into resigning by Nehru. Lockhart's tenure as the Army chief lasted only four and a half months, and he quit his post effective 31 December 1947.

Cunningham's admissions

In the article '1948: The Crucial Year in the History of Jammu and Kashmir', historian Rakesh Ankit reveals Cunningham's diary entries from 6 October 1947 onwards, which establish his involvement with the *kabailis*. Even in his correspondence with Lord Halifax and Lord Mountbatten, he admitted to this fact.

In Bannu, a district in the NWFP, the Political Agent in August 1947 was Arthur Dredge. Dredge worked closely with the Brigade Commander of the Indian Army's Bannu Brigade, Brigadier C.P. Murray. On 19 August 1947, Murray was at Mir Ali Mirali, which is a frontier settlement 41 kilometres away from Bannu. Dredge was the only British officer at work that day in Bannu. Murray was visiting Mir Ali Mirali to review the troops of the 1/8 Punjab Regiment. This battalion had arrived from Bannu in February 1947 to relieve the 14/9 Jat Regiment. It was commanded by Lieutenant Colonel L.J.E. Kealey.

Messervy's secret invasion plan of the Valley is accidentally revealed

A Sikh officer, Major Onkar Singh Kalkat, was in charge of the brigade in the absence of Murray. Both Murray and Kalkat were essentially waiting to hand over the charge of the brigade to Brigadier Mian 'Ganga' Hayauddin of 4/12 Frontier Force Regiment and Major Muhammad Hayat, respectively. On 20 August 1947, a courier arrived, carrying a demi-official letter from General Headquarters (GHQ) in Rawalpindi under the seal of General Frank Messervy. Kalkat opened the letter as he was authorised to do so. Attached to the letter was an appendix entitled 'Operation Gulmarg: The Plan for the Invasion and Capture of Kashmir'. The day for the commencement of the operation was 20 October 1947. At first, Kalkat thought of speaking about the contents of the letter with Dredge, but decided against it. The troubled Kalkat called up Murray and related his startling discovery. Murray reached Bannu the very next day, 21 August 1947, and was also very disturbed after reading the letter. Murray realised that Kalkat's life would be in danger if any non-commissioned Muslim officer or allied staff came to know that he knew about the contents of the Messervy letter.

IMAGE 7.5: General Frank Messervy. Source: Wikipedia

Murray ordered Kalkat to act normally and wait for the handing over to take place on 5 September 1947. Meanwhile, through a network of Muslim friends, which included the District Commissioner of Mian Wali district, Kalkat dispatched his wife and infant son to safety in India. He was left in Bannu, waiting to hand over the charge to his successor. After handing over, the new Brigade Commander, Hayauddin, on some pretext, discreetly put Kalkat on house arrest at Dalipgarh Fort in Bannu.

The head clerk at the brigade HQ had overheard Kalkat talking to Murray; he betrayed Kalkat to the Pakistani military intelligence. However, some of Kalkat's faithful Muslim soldiers, apprehensive that he would be killed, hatched a plan to smuggle him out of town on the night of 22 September 1947. They drove him on a truck to Bannu railway station, from where he took a narrow-gauge train to Mari Indus, a major railhead 150 kilometres away. Mari Indus was the location where Hindus and Sikhs leaving for India were brought in by rail from different parts of the NWFP.

IMAGE 7.6: Major General Onkar Singh Kalkat. Source: Public Domain

However, early next morning, as soon as the duty officer discovered that Kalkat had escaped, he was traced to the town of Mari Indus. The British had established a big Army Service Corps depot at Mari Indus to serve troops stationed in Bannu, Tank, Kohat and Waziristan. Kalkat immediately went to the depot and reported to the British Base Commander that he had handed over the Bannu charge to his successor and was now leaving for India. He feared for his life, he told him, and despite urgent requests from Bannu, the British Base Commander refused to hand him over. The kind British officer provided Kalkat with a rucksack full of provisions and armed him with his own service weapons. Kalkat finally made good his escape by hiding in one of the bogeys of a goods train that was leaving for Amritsar. From there he took another train and arrived in Delhi on 18 October 1947.

The consequences of Kalkat's discovery and his escape from Pakistan

Abdul Qayyum Khan became the Chief Minister of NWFP on 23 August 1947. Only after Khan was sworn in and Cunningham's blessing received, Khan and the Pir of Manki Sharif started mobilising the tribal *lashkars*. This process would take at least three to four weeks.

However, the import of Kalkat's accidental discovery of Messervy's diabolical plan code-named Operation Gulmarg was that it put the British into a tizzy. Since Kalkat had not been physically eliminated yet (he escaped to safety in India), Operation Gulmarg was considered potentially compromised. The plan needed to be salvaged by modifying it so that there was no adverse fallout such as Bacon's nuclear monitoring empire being exposed to public gaze. The weakest link in Operation Gulmarg was the British officers known as District Officers who were to head all units of tribal *lashkars*. The District Officers were in charge of the *khassadars*, or tribal levies, and each officer commanded a *lashkar* of 2,000 men. The approximate strength of the invasion force was 20 British officers and 40,000 *lashkars*. They had been undergoing training for this operation for some time. The tribals were fiercely loyal to the British officers. These officers were men who were made to resign from service and re-employed as private mercenaries, ostensibly recruited by convenient cut-outs like the Pir of Manki Sharif.

These local levies and scouts were not raised for military purposes only. Importantly, they nurtured an intimate bond between the British and a considerable part of the local population. In the course of revisions of levies and scouts, this intimacy was constantly extended. For instance, the time spent with British officers for training was prolonged, the number of scouts under training at one time was reduced and the scouts were converted from part-time to full-time troops. The use of discipline should not be seen primarily as repressive and negative, but as transformative, even educative, enabling the management of the subject population. Members of the scouts and tribal levies were imparted British visions of regularity, order, command and obedience. It was not as if all energy was invested in intangible benefits. Equally significant was material remuneration given to the scouts to compensate for their services, as it made them and their dependents and relatives conscious of the 'boons' of British rule.

It became clear that these British officers, who had developed some kind of symbiotic relationship with the scouts and levies under their command, could not be employed in the invasion, as that would embarrass the Attlee government. Although Kashmir was now legally an 'independent' country, it still housed technically 'illegal' nuclear monitoring facilities unknown to the ruler of the state. And if it acceded to India, it would then become a part of the British Empire, as the King of England was still the sovereign power even though he had lost his title, Emperor of India, on Nehru's insistence. It became a very troublesome issue and was unsatisfactorily resolved by replacing all British-origin *lashkar* commanders with Muslim Pakistani officers. The problem was that while the British officers all spoke Pashto, very few of their available Pakistani replacements knew Pashto. All the replacement officers were overwhelmingly Punjabis. Moreover, none of them could command the loyalty of their men quite like their British predecessors.

Messervy and his cohorts were forced to make the best of a bad deal as events were to later show. The plan was to execute Operation Gulmarg in conjunction, not in isolation, with Operation Datta Khel in Gilgit and an unnamed operation in Poonch to be executed by Sardar Muhammad Ibrahim Khan. This operation also had a British controller whose identity was never revealed. However, suspicion points to the former IG of Police Jammu and Kashmir, Richard Powell, who was sacked from his post in early October after which he went across to Pakistan. It is speculated that the frontman of this operation was Mian Iftikhar Uddin, a wealthy Punjabi politician who was a confidant of Jinnah. Between Sardar Muhammad Ibrahim Khan and his British controller, there were the cut-outs of Mian Iftikhar Uddin and Major Zaman Kiani, formerly of the INA. Kiani had been released from prison in 1946 and was at a loose end. It is unclear how he was drafted into the Poonch operation, but it appears he made his peace with his British captors as he was later appointed Political Agent in Gilgit. That could only have happened if he had the confidence of the British.

The Mir of Hunza rushes back to the Chinese for a second time

After Kashmir became independent, the Mir of Hunza returned to his state in early September 1947. Following his return, he secretly sent envoys to Kashgar with a letter addressed to Zhao Xiguang, the General who had been ousted from Hunza a month earlier by the Gilgit Scouts. His letter was filled with benign pleasantries and a stated desire to restore Hunza's relationship with China. The Mir's envoy, Ali Jauhar, who carried the letter generously, told the Chinese district magistrate at Tashkurgan, the closest border town in Sinkiang, that since Hunza was originally part of the Chinese territory his people were willing to return to China. With those words, Jauhar journeyed to Kashgar, where he arrived in early October, as the guest of Xiguang.

While Jauhar waited patiently in Kashgar, KMT officials in Sinkiang worked furiously to coordinate an ambitious Hunza policy with Nanking, the capital of the KMT government. The idea was to create an arrangement for Nanking to handle all military and foreign affairs of Hunza. Soon, thereafter, Xiguang relayed a message to Nanking on behalf of the Mir, requesting the Chinese troops to be stationed in Hunza. Furthermore, the Mir asked for the implementation of the Xian system of administration in Hunza.

Hari Singh sacks both Scott and Powell

The Maharaja was in a quandary. After he sacked his Prime Minister, Ram Chandra Kak, on 11 August 1947, he discovered that both Richard Powell (IG of Police) and Major General H.L. Scott (C-in-C of Jammu and Kashmir State Forces) were party to Kak and his British wife's escape from Srinagar. If the Maharaja could not trust his own IG and C-in-C, how was he going to preserve the writ of his rule? It is no surprise that less than a month later, on 24 September 1947, Scott relinquished his command. In a few weeks, days before the Pathan invaders reached the state borders, the Maharaja sacked his IG. It is believed that the Maharaja received intelligence reports about Powell's involvement along with his Pakistani counterparts in Muzaffarabad and Rawalpindi. Upon his sacking, Powell left for Rawalpindi via Muzaffarabad, and in no time allegedly joined the Pakistan security apparatus as an advisor.

Brigadier Rajinder Singh was appointed the Chief of Staff of Jammu and Kashmir State Forces on 24 September 1947. Meanwhile, Ismay was in radio contact with Bacon, now the Political Agent in Peshawar. Bacon in turn was in radio contact with Brown in Gilgit. Plans were being crystallised to stage a coup d'état in Gilgit with as little bloodshed and disturbance as possible. The goal was to get the whole Gilgit Agency to accede to Pakistan. The code name of the operation was 'Datta Khel'. Bacon's former Parsee radio operator Limbuwala used one-time pads to communicate with another trusted member of Bacon's team, wireless operator Donaldson. Limbuwala had spent many years in Kashgar as a radio operator and cypher clerk at the British Consulate. He was married to a girl from Kashgar and was in all probability employed by MI 6, as was Donaldson. The operationalisation of Datta Khel was contingent upon Maharaja Hari Singh acceding to India. Brown was strategising his best options.

After the appointment of Mehar Chand Mahajan as the Prime Minister, strong winds were rattling the locks of Sheikh Abdullah's prison cell. As Mahajan began to come to terms with the complexities of his office, he discovered that the Maharaja, through Deputy Prime Minister R.L. Batra, was in serious negotiations with Sheikh Abdullah on the nature of his release. The Maharaja was a beleaguered man and options were fast running out for him. These negotiations culminated in the release of Abdullah on 29 September 1947. However, some weeks before his release, Abdullah was shifted from Bhadarwah Jail of the Doda district in Jammu to the Badami Bagh cantonment hospital in Srinagar. For a few days in the hospital, Abdullah had a regular visitor in the Maharaja's brother-in-law, Nishchant Chand Katoch.

These meetings were to prepare Abdullah for an audience with the Maharaja. A technicality demanded Abdullah to offer the Maharaja *nazar* or a tribute of gold coins. Abdullah had none. So one Shyam Sunder Lal Dhar gave him some gold coins and he presented it to the Maharaja. It appears that some sort of deal was struck between the two men, as a few days later Abdullah was formally released along with other National Conference leaders. The Muslim Conference leaders, however, remained in jail.

Sardar Ibrahim Khan takes control of Poonch

In September 1947, the Poonch uprising acquired a formal command structure under Sardar Muhammad Ibrahim Khan. Weapons were collected, many of them ancient muzzle-loaders, ammunition was prepared and supplies were smuggled across the Jhelum into Poonch and Mirpur, where he had fathered a military organisation of demobilised Poonch soldiers. Soon, a number of Muslim officers in the Jammu and Kashmir state army deserted the Maharaja and joined this force. They were soon followed by volunteers from Pakistan, including several former Muslim INA officers who were looking for action. By 20 October 1947, this force had gained control of almost the entire Poonch district except for the town of Poonch, which was still being garrisoned by the Jammu and Kashmir state forces.

The Valley anticipates an invasion from Pakistan

The first week of October 1947 found the Pakistani government sending Dr Muhammad Din Taseer and Sheikh Sadiq Hassan to convince Abdullah to support Jammu and Kashmir's accession to Pakistan. The Pakistanis were worried that the Maharaja had signed a deal with Abdullah and accession to India was on the cards. Abdullah did not strike a deal with them. He saw no role for himself in a Kashmir that was in Pakistan. Shortly thereafter on 14 October, Abdullah flew to Delhi and stayed with Nehru. Another Pakistani agent provocateur, the Gilgit-born Private Secretary to Jinnah K.H. Khurshid was also in Srinagar, plotting against the Maharaja. As we have seen, mobilisation of the Pashtun tribesmen or *kabailis* took place under the joint leadership of NWFP Chief Minister Abdul Qayyum Khan and the Pir of Manki Sharif. Mian Iftikhar Uddin was the Pakistani puppet master controlling the actions of Sardar Muhammad Ibrahim Khan in Murree.

The tentacles of the Pakistani political machinery extended to the Kashmiri press corps as well. By 7 October 1947, the Maharaja introduced press censorship in the state and ordered the newspaper *Kashmir Times* to stop publishing any news on the state's accession. In protest, the newspaper suspended publication altogether. The *Kashmir Times* was owned and published from Srinagar by Abdul Rahman Mittha, who was a fervent advocate of the state's accession to Pakistan. Since Mittha was not a resident of the state, he was served with an expulsion order and sent over to Pakistan via Kohala. In Pakistan, he joined Sardar Muhammad Ibrahim Khan and started living in Murree. Khan appointed Mittha as the Director of Public Relations in his 'newly formed' government. Ironically, this happened even before the said government was announced.

On 15 October 1947, the new Prime Minister of Jammu and Kashmir, Justice Mehar Chand Mahajan, met a group of Hindu and Sikh refugees who had reached Srinagar by crossing the border at Domel. They reported that they saw large concentrations of tribal Afghans or *kabailis* in the area around Abbottabad and Man Shera. The air was rife with rumours that they were part of the Kashmir Valley invasion plan. On being informed by Mahajan about this development, the Maharaja cabled Attlee, but there was no reaction of any consequence. The Maharaja followed this missive with another written communication on 18 October 1947, this time to Pakistan's Governor-General Jinnah and Prime Minister Liaquat Ali Khan with information about border incursions, subversion of Muslim troops in state forces and other violations of the standstill agreement.

On 18 October 1947, British officers and bureaucrats holidaying with their families in the Valley were given emergency evacuation orders. The very next day, 19 October 1947, 20 RAF buses and trucks from Rawalpindi and Peshawar carried these passengers away from Srinagar to Rawalpindi via Baramulla, Uri and Muzaffarabad. The Maharaja himself was surprised and offended by this unexplained exodus. Clearly, an invasion was imminent. However, the Maharaja was indecisive. To make matters worse, the same day

Liaquat Ali Khan wrote to Mahajan, admonishing the state for trampling on the rights of the state's Muslim majority. This was followed by Jinnah's letter to the Maharaja on 20 October 1947, proposing an end to the acrimony and inviting the Maharaja to send Mahajan to Lahore for amicable talks aimed at settling prickly matters. The Maharaja declined. The following day, the Maharaja and Mahajan made a flash tour of Mirpur district to assess the extent of infiltration along the borders following the fall of Fort Owen.

G.K. Reddy, Resident Editor of *Kashmir Times* in the 1940s, also served as Correspondent for the Associated Press in Srinagar. He used to report to the AP Lahore chief Malik Tajuddin. Reddy was detained at Domel near Muzaffarabad for 10 days in mid-October 1947. After that, he was transported to Kathua, escorted by the military, and expelled from the state at the Pathankot border. The same day, he drove straight to Lahore and reported the whole story to Malik Tajuddin. News of the expulsion of Mittha and Reddy was flashed on Pakistani newspapers and announced on the radio. Sardar Muhammad Ibrahim Khan promptly appointed Reddy as the Deputy Director of Public Relations in the Azad Kashmir government. While in Lahore on 21 October 1947, Reddy received a phone call from Lieutenant Colonel Alavi, Public Relations Officer of the Pakistan Army, who stated that the Ramkot post of the Jammu and Kashmir government was attacked that night. This news, he demanded, should be published as coming from the Azad Kashmir HQ in Pallandri. Reddy was also told that all further news of invasion would come from the Army HQ in Rawalpindi, but

Pallandri is the place that should be mentioned in all press releases.

Major Kalkat shares his intelligence with a sceptical Indian Army

On 18 October 1947, Kalkat arrived in New Delhi. That same day, he met Major General Kulwant Singh and Brigadier P.N. Thapar (later Chief of Army Staff). Kalkat briefed them about the information he had about Operation Gulmarg. Both Thapar and Singh were unconvinced but were duty-bound to take him to meet Defence Minister Sardar Baldev Singh on 19 October. The formal invasion was three days away. A sceptical Baldev Singh asked Thapar, who was from the Army's Intelligence Directorate, to verify Kalkat's account. However, the British-dominated Intelligence Directorate paid no heed to Kalkat's account and therefore no action was taken.

The British deflect the import of Kalkat's intelligence

Instead, Thapar's report to his superior officer was passed up the chain of command to Field Marshall Auchinleck the same day. Auchinleck could not have kept this development from Messervy. A decision was taken between Auchinleck, Messervy and Whitehall to recall Messervy to London for an urgent meeting. Lieutenant General Gracey was ordered to hold the fort in Rawalpindi during Messervy's absence. In London, Messervy met C, Commander Welsh, Chief of the Imperial General Staff Field Marshal Montgomery and officials of the Ministry of Defence. Messervy wanted clear orders on whether to clandestinely orchestrate the *kabaili* invasion. Messervy's orders couldn't have been clearer. He had to ensure the success of the modified Operation Gulmarg so that there was no impediment to the uninhibited and unequivocal functioning of Bacon's nuclear monitoring empire. The Poonch-Muzaffarabad strip had to be taken and secured so that even the remotest possibility of Indian Army artillery guns ever blasting Chaklala airfield was allayed.

But first Messervy would have to return to Rawalpindi via New Delhi and give a public assurance to Mountbatten that no British officers were involved in Operation Gulmarg, and that he had never been the architect of the impending invasion of Kashmir. In his book *Midnight's Furies: The Deadly Legacy of India's Partition*, the author Nisid Hajari reveals that at the end of November 1947 in New Delhi, Messervy swore to Mountbatten he had no involvement in the *kabaili* invasion.

As part of the plan for Operation Gulmarg, Messervy established a special cell at the GHQ Rawalpindi for control and conduct of military operations. This was looked after by the then Director of Military Operations of Pakistan Army Brigadier Sher Khan MC. In the absence of Messervy, Gracey kept in close touch with Sher Khan, who briefed Gracey every morning at the GHQ. There is an interesting revelation by retired Pakistan Army Major General S. Wajahat Husain.

Husain regularly saw Gracey return from GHQ, change into civilian clothes, get into his private car and drive himself over to Sher Khan's office to monitor the Kashmir operations. The field operations were under Major General Loftus Tottenham DSO, MC and GOC 7 Division. Tottenham kept in close touch with Gracey.

Soon after the *kabailis* invaded Kashmir, it became imperative to have some control over them to defend the newly seized area of Azad Kashmir effectively. To that end, Pakistani officer volunteers were inducted immediately to take care of these *lashkars*. This number kept increasing under Colonel Tariq, which is the nom de plume of Colonel Akbar Khan, later Brigadier Akbar Khan. Akbar served under Gracey in his division during the Second World War, and the latter personally selected him to head the *kabaili* invasion force. In fact, after the last battles of Burma, Gracey recommended Akbar Khan for a Victoria Cross (VC) for his bravery, but unfortunately, because of insufficient credible witnesses, Khan only received a Distinguished Service Order (DSO). Gracey proposed and pushed Akbar's name to Liaquat Ali Khan for the leader of the *kabaili* operations in Kashmir.

The reaction of the Indian Army's Intelligence Directorate has to be assessed in the light of other warning signals of the impending invasion that were being flagged in other areas. Given the fast-moving developments in the state, it is incredible that Defence Minister Sardar Baldev Singh not only discounted Major Kalkat's invaluable intelligence but also chose to bury his head in the sand. The extent of British perfidy and its complicity in the grand overall plan to annex the state of Jammu and Kashmir can now be understood and accepted based on these facts. This was complemented by the complacency of Indian politicians like Sardar Baldev Singh. It was only after the invasion started that the import of Kalkat's warning became clear.

On 24 October 1947, he was taken to Nehru to relate his account. Nehru was reportedly livid at Baldev Singh, Thapar and Kulwant Singh, but it was already too late. Even as Nehru was listening to Kalkat's chilling account in New Delhi, in faraway Pallandri, a township in Sudhanoti district, Sardar Muhammad Ibrahim Khan proclaimed the formation of a provincial Azad Jammu and Kashmir government.

IMAGE 7.7: Brigadier Akbar Khan aka Colonel Tariq. Source: Public Domain

The same day, the *kabaili* invasion force overran Muzaffarabad and Uri. The force was bereft of its traditional British leadership; it was now led by Akbar Khan of the Pakistan Army. The *kabailis* destroyed the electricity sub-station at Mahura that supplied power to Srinagar. The city was plunged into an eerie cloak of darkness. In Baramulla, the raiders got side-tracked and began indulging in an orgy of rape, plunder and loot. The road to Srinagar was open and undefended, and the city was theirs for the taking. But the short-sighted *kabailis* ignored the orders of their Punjabi commanders and took to behaving like barbarians. Only after the town had been stripped of its money, firearms, jewellery, women and boys, were the *kabailis* satisfied. The three-day orgy at the prosperous town of Baramulla shook the Maharaja off his inertia. Even the arrival of the Pir of Manki Sharif could not detach the *kabailis* from Baramulla. This loot that had been collected had to be first divided and dispatched to the tribal areas in NWFP. Only then would the marauding force advance to Srinagar. There is no doubt that the ranks of the *kabailis* were buttressed by units and officers from the Frontier Corps and Frontier Constabulary, but the lack of effective and disciplined leadership was their Achilles heel. If the original version of Operation Gulmarg, as was the plan of Operation Datta Khel, had been retained, then the invasion force would have been led by British mercenaries who had resigned their commissions from the Frontier Corps, Frontier Constabulary and the Political Department. This entire force would have been in uniforms and headgear, a little different from the clothing of the ordinary tribesmen.

It is my argument that because of the snafu concerning Kalkat in Bannu, all British mercenaries were asked to stand down. This explains the difference between the success and failure of the invasion. It is also in line with the blueprint of Messervy's Operation Gulmarg that Kalkat studied in Bannu.

When the Maharaja appealed to New Delhi for help on 26 October 1947, he was asked to sign the Instrument of Accession before any help was sent. Meanwhile, near New Delhi, the largest peacetime air armada of 100 planes was being organised by the Government of India to fly off hardened fighting units of the Indian Army to Srinagar once the Instrument of Accession was signed.

Sir V.P. Menon, Principal Secretary to Sardar Patel, flew into Srinagar on 25 October and instructed the Maharaja to leave for Jammu. The Maharaja wanted a 'limited accession' of the state to India, only with regard to defence, foreign affairs and communication. The Maharaja felt vulnerable to being attacked ever since he was betrayed by his army and police chiefs. He wanted the protection of the Indian Army yet retain his hold on the state. Menon flew back to New Delhi with Sheikh Abdullah as the sun descended across the skyline of Srinagar. That night, the Maharaja's entourage left Srinagar for Udhampur with the gold idol of Lord Vishnu, the presiding deity of Gadadhar Temple in Srinagar. According to Sheikh Abdullah, as the caravan of cars drove into Udhampur, the Maharani sat clutching the idol with the car's hood down. This view of the Maharani made all of the Dogra onlookers at Udhampur very angry. Meanwhile, Menon landed in

Jammu and obtained the Maharaja's signature on the Instrument of Accession on the morning of 26 October 1947.

Sheikh Abdullah's first taste of power

After the Maharaja left for the relative safety of Jammu, the morale of Srinagar was very low. If the Indian Army had not arrived by 27 October 1947 and taken charge, anything could have happened in the power vacuum. Sheikh Abdullah, who was in New Delhi, confirmed to both Nehru and Mahajan that he supported the accession. This now paved the way for the creation of a diarchy in the state. On 30 October 1947, the Maharaja appointed Abdullah as the Chief Executive Administrator with Mahajan continuing to function as the Prime Minister.

The Maharaja, now having accepted Abdullah as a political representative of the Muslim majority in his truncated and disintegrating state, opened the way for Mountbatten to play his next card. The argument for a plebiscite was to ascertain what the public wanted. Given that an overwhelming number of the state population was Muslim and a communal conflagration was in progress in the state and neighbouring Punjab, the apprehension in the minds of both Nehru and Patel was that without Sheikh Abdullah on their side, a single comprehensive plebiscite would tilt the scale towards accession to Pakistan. This would include giving away both Jammu and Ladakh, where Muslims were a minority, to Pakistan. The combined numbers in these two regions would be insufficient to fight the Muslim majorities in the Valley, the Poonch belt and the Gilgit Agency. Both Nehru and Patel were unsure if Abdullah wanted to accede to Pakistan. They wanted to be sure that he was on the side of accession to India so that he could bring in the votes from the Valley, the Gilgit and Poonch areas as well in a plebiscite. Therefore, it was necessary to lure and reward Abdullah with political power so that the majority in the state voted for India if ever a plebiscite was called for.

Mountbatten understood this major weakness in the Indian position, and very well so, and his main contribution to the Maharaja's accession may well have been to formally introduce the requirement for a plebiscite and to persuade both Nehru and Patel of its desirability. This was Mountbatten's answer to the commitment he was subjected to by the British deep state. Mountbatten had to frustrate the accession of the state to India. In pursuit of this goal, Mountbatten craftily dragged along both Nehru and Patel. In his radio broadcast on All India Radio on 2 November 1947, Nehru confirmed that the fate of Kashmir is ultimately to be decided by the people and that the pledge India had signed to have a referendum would be fulfilled. Patel may well have been uneasy about the consequences of handing over political power to Abdullah, and he may have preferred an unqualified accession by the Maharaja to India, but Nehru cast his lot with Mountbatten and Patel was overruled. India accepted the principle of the plebiscite. By giving Abdullah the plebiscite card, Nehru had institutionalised its use to prove that the Instrument of Accession was not final in itself.

Chapter 8

Operation Datta Khel

Accession

There was a twist in the execution and acceptance of the Instrument of Accession. Lord Mountbatten accepted the accession but added a caveat to it—the promise of the Indian government to ratify the accession by means of a plebiscite. This implied seeking the consent of the people of the state regarding the accession. Why did Mountbatten enter this caveat? There was no provision under the Indian Independence Act for a sovereign ruler to seek approval or consent of his subjects before deciding to merge with another country, be it India or Pakistan. Why did Nehru and Patel accept it? Was this a last-ditch attempt by Attlee and British Foreign Secretary Ernest Bevin to keep the Kashmir issue alive on international forums forever? It appears that Mountbatten relented to the dictates of the British deep state to plug any loophole that might jeopardise the continued existence of the British nuclear monitoring stations in Gilgit and forcibly yanked Nehru and Patel along.

At this point, one cannot but wonder how and why a standstill agreement between Jammu and Kashmir and the Dominion of India remained unsigned, and who voted against it? If this agreement had been signed at Independence, the Indian government could have come to the aid of the Maharaja much earlier. Perhaps people were told that by signing the agreement, India would be taking a step towards recognising Kashmir's sovereignty and independence. The truth is that not signing a standstill agreement ensured the continued existence of the nuclear monitoring stations in Gilgit. The lack of a standstill agreement did not prevent the Maharaja of Patiala to dispatch a battalion of infantry and a battery of mountain artillery to Kashmir in the first fortnight of October 1947. When Indian troops led by Lieutenant Colonel D.R. Rai landed in Srinagar on 27 October 1947, they found Patiala gunners guarding Srinagar airfield, which had been in their control since 17 October.

Sardar Patel outmanoeuvred

For Patel, the perception of the security challenges facing post-Partition India coincided with the perception of the security challenges facing British India. There was no difference as India had inherited the mantle of power from the British Raj, notwithstanding the creation of the Dominion of Pakistan and its sequestration from the body of India. The Department of External Affairs of the Dominion of India sent a memorandum to British Prime Minister Clement Attlee on 25 October 1947.

This memorandum heavily relied upon conceptual and strategic conclusions drawn from two other Indian government documents of the British era. The first document was a memorandum written by Secretary of External Affairs Caroe on 19 September 1945, in reply to certain queries raised by the new British Foreign Secretary Ernest Bevin. The second was a top-secret memo entitled 'Appreciation of the scale of direct military assistance which could be provided in support of Tibet' prepared by the British General Staff in 1946.

Geopolitically, as mentioned in the Department of External Affairs memorandum of 25 October 1947, India was just about to suffer a major defeat just like the defeat of the British in Afghanistan in 1841–1842. The Gilgit Agency, which was the key to the defence of the western end of the northern frontier, a crucial zone where Afghanistan, Russia and China meet, was almost slipping away from the control of Jammu and Kashmir. It seemed like it was going to be formally placed under the flag of Pakistan in less than a week. Consequently, India's north-west frontier was pushed several hundred miles to the east and a century of British strategic planning, including the sale of Kashmir to Gulab Singh in 1846, was undone. The real goal of the military intervention that began on 27 October 1947 was to gain control over not the Valley of Kashmir but the Gilgit Agency.

The memorandum of 25 October 1947 makes it clear that the state of Jammu and Kashmir was of fundamental importance to India, and that had nothing to do with the fact that it was Nehru's ancestral home. The legal merits of the Maharaja's Instrument of Accession were also not the main reason for the state's significance for India. It was the symbol of India's status as the true successor to the British Raj.

The announcement of this memorandum, possibly inspired by Sardar Patel, was in congruence with the interests of the British deep state. However, unless Patel was made the Prime Minister of India, the British deep state doubted that India could be relied upon to deliver on Britain's strategic interests. That was the paradox that caused the British the anxiety to immediately execute Operation Datta Khel to thwart the realisation of Patel's strategic vision for the defence of the Dominion of India.

Gilgit erupts

Around this time, frequent cypher messages were being exchanged between the newly promoted Colonel Bacon in Peshawar and Major Brown in Gilgit. Because of what happened with Kalkat, the British mercenaries had to stand down, and the opportunity for a clean takeover of Srinagar and the entire Valley was lost forever. Pax Britannica failed, so they had to resort to the use of communal arms to achieve its ends. Bacon was concerned that matters in Gilgit would get similarly messy. On 28 October 1947, Brown received word that the Mehtar of Chitral was mobilising forces to join his proposed joint command, which was planning to put up a stiff guerrilla resistance to an expected ascent by the Indian Army. Similarly, the forces of the Wali of Swat entered Tangir and were posted on the borders of the Gilgit Agency. On 29 October 1947, at the instructions of Bacon, Brown readied for the execution of a bloodless coup by providing Governor Ghansara

Singh with a chance to step down and promising him a safe passage out of Gilgit. Brown told the Governor the next day that the alternative was for him to hold a referendum in the Gilgit Agency.

This was along the lines of the referendum suggested by Mountbatten for the entire state. That way, Ghansara Singh could continue to govern the province till the requisite authority took over. Singh disagreed as both these options not only offended his Dogra pride but were also regarded as acts of treason against the Maharaja. As a result, Brown had no choice but to put into execution Operation Datta Khel on the night of 31 October 1947.

Brown laid siege to the Governor's residence that night, and after a fierce gun battle, Ghansara Singh and his staff were outnumbered and forced to surrender. The next morning, 1 November 1947, Brown sent cypher messages by radio to Abdul Qayyum Khan and Bacon, informing them that he was now the pro tem administrator of Gilgit. Brown's message to Abdul Qayyum Khan was carefully worded, dispelling the notion that the coup d'état was instigated by the British government. Now that the power had passed to Brown, it had to be held and preserved until it could be passed on to the Government of Pakistan and permanently secured in their favour. Further, plans had to be implemented on how to keep the Indian Army at bay. Brown had no remorse. He had committed treason against the state of Jammu and Kashmir after taking an oath to uphold the state's constitution and the rule of the Maharaja. He had drawn generous pay and allowances and had confiscated 60,000 pounds from the state's funds lying in the treasury at Gilgit. There is unsubstantiated evidence to suggest there was much more money in the treasury and that it was never accounted for.

He deserted, mutinied against and instigated the Gilgit Scouts. He also ordered the scouts to finish off large parts of the Maharaja's forces by deceit. Since the state of Jammu and Kashmir acceded to and was accepted by India, which was then a Dominion of the British Empire, his actions amounted to waging war against the King and high treason. Not only Brown but many others, including Mathieson, Bacon, Cunningham, Messervy and Ismay, had committed high treason against the throne. This is the irony behind the operations Gulmarg and Datta Khel.

IMAGE 8.1: Governor of Gilgit Brigadier Ghansara Singh looking at his watch. Source: Public Domain

On 4 November 1947, an imprisoned and humiliated Ghansara Singh signed a surrender order drafted by Brown. Thereafter, Brown exchanged numerous radio messages with Bacon about the military challenges created by the Indian Army's presence in the state. From Harmosh near Kargil to Gilgit, the Burzil Pass was the weakest link on Astore Road. This position was reinforced. In the event of the Indian Army taking this route, guerrilla action would be launched between Astore and Ramghat. More scouts were urgently recruited and trained; they were drawn from the Chitral, Hunza and Ishkoman forces. Contact was made with General Tariq, instructing him to secure the Gurez Valley to prevent the Indian force from coming up the Burzil route. In fact, a year later in November 1948, Brigadier Kanhaiya Lal 'Bagga' Atal, Commander of the 77 Para Brigade, took Kargil and was ready to go up the Astore Road to Gilgit. He signalled to the Northern Command HQ, asking for permission to do so. The permission was never granted. Why?

Back in Gilgit on 11 November 1947, Brown received a cypher message from Bacon in Peshawar, informing him that a representative from Pakistan was arriving on 16 November to relieve Brown of his command. Bacon wanted all the Rajas and Mirs of the Gilgit Agency to be in Gilgit to meet this representative of the Pakistan government.

On 16 November, at exactly 10:00 AM, a Harvard aircraft of the Royal Pakistan Air Force (RPAF), flown by Squadron Leader Ahmed, landed in Gilgit and delivered the new Political Agent Mohammad Alam. Alam had been thoroughly briefed by Bacon in Peshawar before flying to Gilgit. Earlier he was a sub-collector or tehsildar in NWFP. The handover was formalised on 17 November 1947 and the Pakistani flag was slowly hoisted on the flagstaff, reaching the pole-head on the last bar of 'God Save the King'. Thereafter, as per Bacon's instructions, over the next week, plans were put into place for formalising recruitment of additional scouts, organising their training and ensuring their equipment from wireless radios, automatic weapons to pack mules. On 24 November 1947, Bacon ordered Brown to appear at Peshawar for briefings.

Brown briefs his bosses in Peshawar

The same Harvard aircraft piloted by the same Squadron Leader, Ahmed, flew Brown to Peshawar on 25 November 1947. On landing in Peshawar, Brown was driven up to Khyber House, the residence of Colonel Roger Bacon. After being debriefed by the Colonel, the two of them drove over to the Government House to meet NWFP Governor Sir George Cunningham for the most important debriefing. Brown was asked to prepare a detailed report along with maps of ground positions. He was also met by Charles Duke, the British Deputy High Commissioner in Peshawar and former Political Agent in South Waziristan. Duke was also given a copy of the Brown report, which was forwarded to Whitehall.

IMAGE 8.2: Former President of Pakistan Iskander Mirza. Source: Public Domain

Bacon also called his old friend Lieutenant Colonel Iskander Mirza from Sandhurst, who was Pakistan's Defence Secretary and later Pakistan's President, and asked him to fly into Peshawar to meet Brown. Brown and Bacon both briefed Mirza. A British mercenary who had waged war against the King came in from the cold and was warmly received back in the folds of the British deep state. Such was the treachery at hand in the execution of all the variants of operations Gulmarg and Datta Khel.

Further, when Brown transferred power to the new Pakistani Political Agent Mohammad Alam in Gilgit, he simultaneously commenced tripartite negotiations with the Mir and Alam of Hunza to merge with Pakistan. British intelligence in both Kashgar and Nanking confirmed the import of the rapidly developing process taking place concurrently in Kashgar and Nanking. These negotiations were inconclusive when Brown left for Peshawar. The Mir of Hunza refused to relent as he was negotiating for the best deal possible. He adroitly played his China card to the hilt.

The troublesome Mir of Hunza continues to play his China card

While Brown was in Peshawar, on 4 December 1947 General Zhao received Nanjing's encouragement to negotiate with the Mir's envoys on the following Four-Point Principle:

(1) The status of Hunza should be confirmed as an inalienable part of the Chinese territory.
(2) The Hunza state should be transformed into an 'autonomous district' under the legal jurisdiction of the Sinkiang Provincial government.
(3) Mohammad Jamal Khan, Mir of Hunza, would continue to hold his hereditary title and would concurrently serve as Administrative Commissioner of the newly created Hunza autonomous district.
(4) Whereas the Mir of Hunza would remain in authority to deal with Hunza's internal affairs, the foreign and military affairs of Hunza should be dominated by the Chinese central government.

By the time the negotiations in Kashgar between Chinese officials and Hunza envoys almost reached an agreement, the coup in Gilgit became world news. Suddenly, Nanjing ordered General Zhao to cease negotiations, but he ignored the order.

A worried Cunningham ordered Brown to fly back to Gilgit post-haste to restrain the Mir from his posture of adventurous brinkmanship. Clearly, the new Political Agent Mohammad Alam was at sea in his seemingly futile negotiations with the Mir of Hunza. Cunningham also worked the wires and spoke to C. C in turn spoke to Mao Renfeng, the successor to the legendary KMT spymaster Dai Li. Mao Renfeng agreed to order Zhao to lay off Hunza for now. It was only after Brown's return to Gilgit in December 1947 and all the loose ends were tied up that the Mir of Hunza rescinded on 28 December 1947 his merger with China and threw in his lot with Pakistan.

But Zhao had his finger on the pulse of the state. Opportunities still existed. On 7 January 1948, six days after the 1 January international declaration of the first Indo-Pak War, General Zhao and the Mir of Hunza's envoys signed a modus vivendi, an agreement allowing conflicting parties to coexist peacefully either indefinitely or until a final settlement is reached. Although the General argued that the envoys' consent to the document 'implied that theoretically, the Hunza state would henceforth be ready to come under Nationalist China's administrative jurisdiction and recognise China's "suzerainty", if not sovereignty', nonetheless, he lacked the Mir's certification. In February and again in June 1948, Zhao sent envoys to gain Mir Jamal Khan's signature to the Four-Point Principle, which 'the shrewd Mir turned down'.

The British secure their interests through their proxy

The Indus that flowed through Ladakh-Baltistan-Gilgit was extremely important for the survival of the people of Pakistan. The corollary of Operation Datta Khel was that the takeover of the Gilgit Agency would provide Pakistan with a means to outflank India in the race for Ladakh and the waters of the Indus. Only a week after the memorandum of 25 October 1947 was sent to Attlee, Mountbatten and Ismay flew to Lahore to discuss the Kashmir crisis with Jinnah and Liaquat Ali Khan. This summit was inconclusive. Ismay was put in the uncomfortable position of opposing the party line of the British deep state. Liaquat Ali Khan visited New Delhi in December 1947, and Mountbatten, Nehru, Baldev Singh and Ayyangar followed him to Lahore. For a plebiscite to happen, Pakistan needed the Indian Army to withdraw and then have a 'neutral' caretaker government to replace the Mahajan-Abdullah diarchy. By now, post-Operation Datta Khel, the Government of India was convinced that the Pakistani government had officially sponsored both the operations. What was still unknown or unspoken was the perfidy by which the British used their newly created proxy in the form of Pakistan to invade the state and separate those parts vital to the functioning of Bacon's nuclear monitoring empire.

During the last two months of 1947, the Indian Army succeeded in breaking the backs of the raiders and securing Srinagar.

IMAGE 8.3: Major General Kulwant Singh at a forward post in Kashmir during the First Kashmir War, 1947–1949. Source: Public Domain

Army HQ in New Delhi created a new command based in Jammu called HQ Jammu and Kashmir Force. The same Kulwant Singh who was sceptical of Kalkat's intelligence inputs days earlier was given this command. He arrived in Srinagar on 5 November 1947. However, Kulwant Singh was to discover that the biggest obstacle to his job of throwing out the *kabailis* was the Mountbatten-Lockhart-Bucher triumvirate. On Mountbatten's orders, Nehru had to restrain Kulwant Singh from recovering the Gilgit Agency and the Muzaffarabad-Poonch belt. On 1 January 1948, India put forth its case before the Security Council of the UN.

The end of the farce of the 'Supreme HQ'

The Messervy plan and the invasions of the Valley and Poonch, as well as the coup in Gilgit, clearly showed that the Supreme Commander's HQ of the Joint Defence Council of India and Pakistan in New Delhi was spinning out of control. It was set up to ensure the smooth division of the Armed Forces of unified India and its assets between the two new Dominions. It was based in New Delhi and staffed entirely by British officers with Field Marshall Claude Auchinleck as the Supreme Commander.

The irony is that Auchinleck was commissioned in 1903 in the Indian Army, and he joined the 62nd Punjabis in April 1904. He was a fluent Punjabi speaker and had mastered all the dialects of Punjabi spoken in different Doabs. The rumour was that he knew his men a bit too well as there were unproven allusions to his choice of sexuality. If anyone knew India, particularly Punjab, it was Auchinleck. It is unlikely that Messervy could have drawn up his invasion plan under the aegis of Operation Gulmarg without Auchinleck knowing of it.

Furthermore, since Auchinleck was C-in-C of the Indian Army before becoming the Supreme Commander of India and Pakistan, it is highly unlikely that Messervy, who headed the Northern Command and reported to Auchinleck, could have drastically reorganised his command on 23 July 1947 for creating the grounds for the invasion of Kashmir a few months later. Nor could Auchinleck have been unaware of the frontier committee created in 1944 and headed by Lieutenant

General Francis Tucker, which recommended the withdrawal of regular Indian Army troops from the Razmak, Wana and Khyber Pass garrisons to be replaced with scouts and *khassadars*. Cunningham and Caroe both recommended immediate implementation of these recommendations. The immediate effect of this was to remove all Hindu and Sikh army officers and soldiers from the NWFP and have the northern frontiers of India defended by the Muslim-only Frontier Scouts and Frontier Constabulary.

The Supreme Commander's HQ was supposed to be a neutral body. It owed its loyalty to both India and Pakistan. As Supreme Commander, Auchinleck had free access to the HQ of both Indian and Pakistan Armies. He was in constant touch with the chiefs of both Armies. Moreover, he was opposed to Partition, which he thought was a fundamentally dishonourable policy. He also refused a peerage to distance himself from being construed as a votary of Partition.

The inescapable conclusion is that Auchinleck was a party to the invasion of Kashmir, although he may have been a silent and passive participant. However, his conscience probably got the better of him that he recommended the dissolution of his command in early November 1947. He probably felt it was too absurd for him to continue in office after the two invasions and the Gilgit coup. Moreover, he drastically lost the confidence of the Union cabinet. A communiqué issued on 10 November 1947 formally outlined the dissolution of Auchinleck's command on 30 November 1947.

He left India on 1 December 1947. Auchinleck was an honourable soldier, and he probably knew that his legacy had been tarred by his unwitting participation in such a monumental farce.

Brown is rewarded

This story has an interesting postscript. After his return from Gilgit in the middle of January 1948, William Brown, who was still employed by Commander Welsh's unit TAL buried within the deep folds of MI6, was appointed to the Frontier Constabulary, the police force of the NWFP in Pakistan, as part of a new cover appointment. In July 1948, Brown while still a member of the Frontier Constabulary was awarded the Member of British Empire (MBE) by the King-Emperor with an unspecified citation. Now, awarding an MBE to Brown was one of the abiding paradoxes of British rule in the Indian subcontinent because he had not only resigned his commission in the Army but had also waged war against the King-Emperor. This confirms that operations Gulmarg and Datta Khel were both the brainchildren of the British deep state, and the operations were successful to the extent that they were able to preserve British control over parts of Jammu and Kashmir despite its accession to India.

Chapter 9

The British Get Enmeshed in Kashmir

A breakthrough in Soviet atom bomb project

On 8 December 1944, the mining and processing of uranium was transferred to the exclusive jurisdiction of the NKVD, the Soviet secret service agency. Following this directive, uranium mining commenced vigorously in Soviet Central Asia, including in Sinkiang. The Sinkiang site had the major share of the deposits. On 15 May 1945, the Mining and Chemical Combine6 was established to extract and process uranium and uranium deposits from this region. On 8 September, the NKVD decided to permit former Nazi scientists—Gustav Hertz, Von Ardenne, Robert Dopel, Peter Adolf Thiessen, Max Volmer and Nikolaus Riehl among others—who had security clearances to join this monumental project. By December 1945, Kurchatov had all the uranium and graphite needed and the research reactor F-1 was completed. The reactor was loaded with 45 tons of uranium and 400 tons of graphite. By July 1946, Combine6 was operating in full swing at its location about four kilometres from Khojand in Soviet Tajikistan. On Christmas Day in 1946, Kurchatov started the reactor and achieved a self-sustaining nuclear reaction. The bomb became a reality and its success was credited to Beria. The commencement of the nuclear reaction was viewed with alarm at the British Gen 163 Cabinet committee meeting in London on 8 January 1947.

By July 1948, Combine6 had extracted 250,000 tons of uranium ore and produced 135 tons of uranium. The problem was that while Enrico Fermi's research reactor SR-1 in Chicago only needed 6 tons of uranium blocks, Kurchatov's F-1 reactor needed around 45 tons of uranium blocks. Therefore, much greater quantities of uranium ore were needed to make the first Soviet reactor F-1 critical, than had been the case in the US for its reactor SR-1. Khojand, the location of Combine6, was less than an hour's flying time from RAF Chaklala in Rawalpindi and well within the range of RAF reconnaissance aircraft. Sidney Cotton was hard at work.

The British perspective on the fighting in Kashmir

The fighting in Kashmir continued unabated throughout 1948. The Indian C-in-C General Robert Lockhart was pro-Pakistan in his outlook, as was his successor General Bucher. All through 1948, Bucher would moderate military decisions taken by other Indian officers. This was primarily to please the orders from London and to ensure that British interests were not unduly harmed as a result of the fighting. No one knew the truth about the war started by the British for the British. He also empathised with Pakistan's vital need for Kashmir in terms of defence, water supplies and the need to control the NWFP.

These two Generals were strongly supported by West Punjab Governor Sir Robert Francis Mudie. Mudie attended school with Cunningham and Lockhart, and after reuniting in India, they were all a part of the British deep state that thought it necessary for Pakistan to retain a post-Partition presence in the part of India that contained Kashmir and the NWFP. Mudie anticipated three threats to Pakistan's existence, namely the Afghan-Russia threat, the India-Abdul Ghaffar Khan threat and the conflict in Kashmir. He was of the view that Pakistan was the only barrier to the spread of communism in the subcontinent.

Another famous officer of the Pakistan Army, Major General W.J. Cawthorn, very lucidly voiced all the British strategic fears arising from the Kashmir dispute. In his speech in London's Chatham House in 1948, he argued that Pakistan could not afford to have a hostile India by the western borders of Jammu and Kashmir. Such a scenario would bring the Indian Army within 30 miles of the Pakistan Army HQ in Rawalpindi, right behind its vital north-south communication line. It would give India control over the waters of Chenab, Jhelum and Indus rivers and put India in direct contact with Afghanistan, Chitral and Swat. There was already speculation that the Indian National Congress and the Young Afghan Party were jointly encouraging the Pashtunistan idea. It would also provide India with a land border with the USSR.

RIAF was sparingly deployed in Kashmir because of British restraints

The total aircraft strength of the RIAF at that time was 48 piston-engine Tempest fighter bombers, 20 Spitfire fighters and 7 Dakota transports. An Infantry Brigade was to be airlifted to Srinagar. The Dakotas did the transportation while Tempests and Spitfires provided the necessary close air support to the Army. In December 1947, Air Commodore Mehar Singh created a sort of record by landing a Dakota with three tons of load against the rated normal load of one ton at the newly constructed airstrip at Poonch. In six days, the No. 12 Squadron of the RIAF carried out 73 sorties, averaging more than 2 sorties per aircraft per day, carrying more than 210 tons of supplies to Poonch and evacuating thousands of refugees during the return journeys.

Spitfires based at Ambala were shifted to Srinagar on 30 October 1947 and were soon engaged in the strafing of *kabailis* beyond Patan. Within a week of the commencement of air operations, Tempests from No. 7 Squadron ex-Ambala were instrumental in ensuring victory in the battle of Shelatang. The Tempests were involved in repeated attacks and tactical recce missions over Naushera, Poonch, Rajouri, Jhangar and Handover areas, causing heavy damage to enemy strongholds. The strikes over vital enemy strongholds in Pallandri, Domel and at the Kishan Ganga Bridge had effectively stopped enemy troop movements and literally paralysed them.

IMAGE 9.1: Air Commodore Baba Mehar Singh, IAF. Source: Public Domain

On 4 May 1948, Mehar Singh led six Dakotas of No. 12 Squadron from Srinagar to Leh, zipping across high mountain ranges of the Himalayas, flying at up to 24,000 feet, negotiating the Zojila and Fatula Passes and landing at an improvised sandy airstrip next to the Indus River at a height of 11,540 feet. Major General Thimayya was Singh's passenger on the principal Dakota. From 28 May onwards, braving all odds, No. 12 Squadron flew in armed soldiers, food supplies, tents, equipment and medical stores before the enemy arrived three days later. No. 12 Squadron flew 700

sorties and airlifted 1,000 tons of stores during the airbridge operations from Srinagar to Leh.

British overflights above Soviet Russia from Chaklala outsourced to mercenary pilots from Poland

By early 1948, the relatively unsuccessful Operation Gulmarg and the increasing knowledge of the participation of British officers in the conflict brought to light another worrying aspect of the British presence in Pakistan. There was the risk of intense embarrassment if any of the RAF Lincoln bombers based at Chaklala or the RAF Halifax bombers based at both Chaklala and Risalpur was shot down over the Soviet Union during their many overflights and the aircrew captured. Also, if any British pilots in the RPAF were shot down in combat dogfights with RIAF pilots, there would be a massive outcry in the press and House of Commons. It was important to transfer these flights to be operated by non-Commonwealth but trained and trusted European-origin pilots employed by the RPAF.

The then RAF chief of the Joint Photographic Air Intelligence Board, Air Vice Marshal Lawrence Pendred, discovered a unique solution to this challenge. There were two RAF bomber squadrons staffed by Polish-origin officers, aircrew and ground staff. These were No. 300 and 301 Polish Bomber Squadrons. Both these squadrons were flying long-range Halifax bombers but the Polish-origin pilots and ground crew had been unemployed as the squadrons were disbanded.

IMAGE 9.2: Air Commodore W.J.M. Turowicz, PAF. Source: Wikipedia

Altogether 30 Polish-origin ex-RAF pilots and 16 ex-RAF ground crew, largely drawn from the Polish-staffed disbanded RAF squadrons No. 300 and 301, and C flight of No. 138 Squadron that was flying Halifax bombers reconfigured as transports and used for special operations, were induced to move to Pakistan with the RPAF. The pilots of RAF No. 138 Squadron had specially flown the Halifax for the Special Operations Executive and were very familiar with flying special operations. The Polish contingent was commanded by RAF Squadron Leader Wladyslaw Turowicz. Turowicz was an accomplished Halifax pilot during the Second World War. These Polish pilots were absorbed to RAF Chaklala and RAF Risalpur to fly the Halifax bombers that originally belonged to RAF No. 298 Squadron.

Interestingly, Pendred's predecessor at the Joint Photographic Air Intelligence Board was Air Marshall Thomas Walker Elmhirst, then IAF chief. After serving his term as the C-in-C of IAF, Elmhirst was posted to Emu Field in Australia to run Operation Totem, the first British atmospheric nuclear tests, in October 1953. It's no coincidence that Elmhirst was posted in India during this critical period to ensure that the RIAF did not engage either RAF or RPAF aircraft involved in operations over the Soviet Union. The British tried as far as possible to tie up all loose ends.

British partisanship towards Pakistan is exposed

On 11 February 1948, Lieutenant General Douglas Gracey took over as Pakistan Army chief from General Frank Messervy, the architect of Operation Gulmarg. It is pertinent to point out that Gracey was selected as C-in-C by Jinnah himself from the names put up by the British. The shortlisted names were Gracey and Tucker. Jinnah had known Gracey for a long time. He was also the Indian I Corps Commander in Karachi, living in Quaid-e-Azam House before Partition. Jinnah had full confidence in his judgment. Gracey had the confidence of not only Jinnah but Liaquat Ali Khan as well and was also given a year's extension after the first Pakistani C-in-C-designate General Iftikhar's unfortunate death in an air crash.

Gracey had to gear himself up for India's forthcoming spring offensive expected to commence in March 1948, once the snows had partially melted. Bucher and

Gracey viewed this as a decisive thrust at Pakistan's jugular. Both the British Generals almost comically orchestrated the adoption of mutually defensive positions. This is best highlighted in the memoirs of Major General Loftus Tottenham, famously known in the British Army by the nickname Black Tarantula. Tottenham was a Division Commander in the Pakistan Army during this war. He commented that the Kashmir war was strange in that it was fought under several restrictions. The prevalent attitude amongst the British officers in the Pakistan Army was to hit the Indians hard but not too hard, otherwise, they knew, there would be all kinds of unsavoury consequences. The same view prevailed on the other side. It was a shadow boxing competition with both boxers tied to a leash.

The Pakistanis seemed to have decided to use the opportunity to secure control over the Indian Territory through which the rivers Chenab, Jhelum and Indus flow into Pakistan. To them, this was an opening to be exploited to the hilt. In fact, Hodson relates that in April 1948, the East Punjab government curtailed the supply of water to West Punjab pending settlement of how the water should be paid for. Thereafter, at an Indo-Pak ministerial meeting on 3 May 1948, Dr Ambedkar who represented India insisted that no water could be supplied unless Pakistan accepted India's ownership of the water. The Pakistani Minister Ghulam Mohammed met Lord Mountbatten at the end of the inconclusive meeting and berated Dr Ambedkar's stance. Hodson relates that Mountbatten immediately phoned Nehru who agreed to open the taps.

Here was the irony of it all. Pakistan invades Kashmir and is at war with India, but the Governor-General of India orders his government to continue to supply free water to Pakistan!

In early May 1948, the British High Commissioner in Pakistan Laurence Grafftey-Smith informed Whitehall of the presence of Pakistan Army troops in Kashmir. Of greater concern was his revelation that two British officers in the Pakistan Army—Lieutenant Colonel Milne and Captain Skellon—were operating in Kashmir with Gracey's approval. He also reported that three Pakistani battalions were present in Kashmir, and the opposing Indian Commanders were aware of this yet continued to avoid direct engagement. Intriguingly, Gracey had personally informed Bucher about the officers being present in the theatre of fighting. Whitehall worried that this could prove to be a big embarrassment if the information leaked out. However, one month later in June 1948, the presence of regular Pakistani troops in Kashmir was evident beyond any doubt. Two Dominions of the Empire were at war with each other and there were British officers pitted against one another.

On 22 May 1948, 7 Sikh, supported by the armoured cars of C Squadron of 7 Cavalry, captured the territory up to Nawa Rundan Nala and MS 68 on the south bank of Jhelum from 1/13 Frontier Force Rifles. It was only after 7 Sikh captured a POW and produced the remnants of a 4.2-inch Howitzer bomb fired at them that the Army HQ was convinced that the regular Pakistan Army had joined in the conflict in Jammu and Kashmir. This was key evidence.

All of this evidence of the complicity of British-officered Pakistani Army units actively engaging in the fighting in Kashmir caused much embarrassment to Mountbatten. He was, after all, a member of the ruling British royal family and a cousin of King George VI. In these circumstances, worried that his continuation as Governor-General of India would not only cause acute embarrassment to the British government but also tarnish his own public image, not to speak of his legacy, Mountbatten decided to resign. He quit his post on 21 June 1948.

During the summer of 1948, Gracey prepared plans to launch fresh limited offensives in Kashmir against the Indian Army to halt its advance. The execution of the plan included for the first time heavily concentrated artillery bombardment of the Indian Army's sensitive lines of communications across the border in the Beripatan and Naushera areas. On the evening of 23 July 1948, the Pakistan Army started concentrated shelling at Jhangar near Naushera. The artillery fire was accurate, heavy and caused severe damage to the 4th Divisional HQ leading to the death of Brigadier Usman Shah, officiating Division Commander. Shah had successfully launched Operation Kipper to secure Kot. A week later, a mixed force of 10,000 Pakistani soldiers and irregulars attacked Naushera. The attack was repulsed and 900 Pakistanis were killed. The shelling of the Divisional HQ commenced just after the evening namaz prayers. The Pakistani's baited Shah because they knew he would break cover and order retaliatory shelling and, in the process, endanger his life.

They knew that Shah always fought on the front foot. That was exactly what happened.

British Foreign Secretary Ernest Bevan decided not to take any action about the direct involvement of British officers in the conflict. His colleague, the Defence Secretary, and the Chiefs of Staff Committee also kept mum. The reason the British were playing possum was very clear—if India asked British officers to step down, the Pakistan Army would be crippled from lack of senior officers. How would the Indians be prevented from retaking Gilgit then? In India, General Bucher put a lid on this issue and acquiesced to orders from Whitehall to stall any plans for offensive action against Pakistani forces. He also toned down the plans for the use of RIAF, which was proposed by Indian Generals. Bucher was the Trojan horse in the Indian Army who, in hindsight, deserved to be charged with high treason.

In London, the Foreign Office was primed to resolve and resist all Indian enquiries on this subject by bluffing and presenting every argument that they could muster. The reason for this was that Gracey was stubbornly opposed to stepping down and was not bothered about embarrassing the British government in the process. Gracey's zealousness had no boundaries. In July 1948, Whitehall was further shocked to learn that a dozen British officers from the Pakistan Army were fighting in actual ground combat in Kashmir. India, on the other hand, was restrained by Bucher as he was anxious about going into direct combat with Pakistan. He used his influence to stop moderating and to diminish the initiatives of Indian Commanders on the field and at the planning level.

While in office, Mountbatten encouraged Bucher and Elmhirst to remain in personal touch with Nehru and manipulate him from taking any aggressive action that might put Pakistan at risk. The fear was that any use of the RIAF could lead to air attacks on the key airfields of Chaklala in Rawalpindi and Risalpur. These airfields were vital for both the RAF overflights above the Soviet Union and the RAF flights that carried various samples of uranium ore to the UK, which were ferried into the Gilgit Agency by British agents in Sinkiang. Furthermore, the RIAF was to be restrained from attacking Gilgit for fear of inadvertently destroying British assets there. Bucher's focus was to deflect the Army from taking the war into the Gilgit Agency and to actively thwart any attempt to retake Gilgit.

Bucher constantly harped on having military operations that are linked to political policies. Unless the Government of India spelt out its political objectives vis-à-vis Pakistan, how could he order appropriate military action? However, Gracey's aggressive policy for the Pakistan Army soon faced repercussions. One of the British officers in the Pakistan Army fighting in Kashmir's Tithwal sector, Major R.E. Sloan, was killed on 10 July 1948. He was killed while commanding 71 Field Company of the Royal Pakistan Engineers. Whitehall strove to hush this mishap. Secretary of State for Commonwealth Affairs Philip Noel-Baker advised Attlee against enforcing the stepping down of officers, and argued that it would remove the influence of moderation by India and would be impossible for Pakistan to run its Army without British officers. How would Gilgit be defended in that case? Noel-Baker was supported by Grafftey-Smith who delivered false assurance that no British officer would be posted on actual battlefields in Kashmir thereafter.

As a result, a brazen and trite Attlee turned down Nehru's request for a stand-down of British officers by arguing that all errant British officers who had participated in the fighting would be recalled immediately. Gracey was made the scapegoat by Whitehall, calling him names and charging him with disloyalty to the British Crown. Quite a performance indeed!

Operation Fitzwilliam

Meanwhile, by March 1948, the beginnings of an institutional framework for detecting Soviet nuclear tests were put into place under the aegis of an Anglo-US programme called Operation Fitzwilliam. This included aerial scientific surveillance of any enterprises directly involved in the processes supporting the Soviet atomic programme through the detection and measurement of the radioactive gas content of the atmosphere and by flight fitted with detection instruments. The Polish-flown Halifax bombers began flying regular sorties over Khojand's Combine6.

Murkier waters

Neither Grafftey-Smith's nor Noel-Baker's false assurances could be upheld by a desperate Pakistani Army. British officers continued to lead their Pakistani troops against the Indian Army. A month after his first request, in August 1948, Nehru once again requested a stand-down of British officers from both Armies. This time, the request was routed by Nehru through the Chancellor of the Exchequer Stafford Cripps and Lord Ismay. Both Noel-Baker and Bevin, however, argued that the Pakistan Army would disintegrate without British officers. Pakistan was not only in the frontline against Soviet expansion but also held great leverage in the Muslim world. Furthermore, the UN, which was now playing a significant role in the Kashmir conflict, viewed all British officers as a great stabilising influence. By this time, the Indian Armed Forces had less than half of the 800-odd British personnel who were working for the Pakistan Armed Forces. Lastly, the treasonous link between Bucher and Gracey would have snapped had the stand-down been declared. Therefore, Attlee refused Nehru's request, citing a combination of desperation and disillusionment in Pakistan, defiance by British officers there, Muslim hostility and communist profit.

Four months later, for a third time, a frustrated Nehru raised the issue of a stand-down with Attlee and received his third successive refusal, this time communicated via the British Defence Secretary.

By now, the entire rank of British officers in the Pakistan Army was fully engaged in the war. Meanwhile, to buy time, the British government commissioned the Director of Military Intelligence Lieutenant General Sir Gerard Templer to write what was commonly referred to as the Templer Report. In November 1948, this report confirmed that 440 British officers served in executive positions in Pakistan as opposed to the 230 Britons in India. The contrast in this imbalance was exacerbated by Bucher's relative detachment from the war as against Gracey's hands-on involvement in it. The choice before the British now was to stand-down or ceasefire as fighting the Indian Army was a losing proposition. Let alone winning territorial control over the three Kashmiri rivers, the issue was being thrown out of the Gilgit Agency and out of the nuclear race as well. To protect their assets in the Gilgit Agency, the British would probably have to go to war against India.

Just before the Templer Report was commissioned, on 1 November 1948 an Indian brigade group supported by 7 Cavalry comprising Stuart tanks broke through the Zojila Pass and relentlessly drove out the Pakistani invaders from the Ladakh district. In the history of warfare, Zojila was the highest point where tanks were used. The implication of this move was both tactical and strategic. Tactically, it opened up the route to take Leh in the east. Strategically, it threatened Kargil, Skardu and Gilgit in the north. These developments alarmed Gracey. He felt that both Swat and Chitral were also vulnerable as there was a potential Indian fifth column in the NWFP. Governor Caroe also sounded the warning bell as did Commander Welsh in London.

Earlier in August 1948, the United Nations Commission for India and Pakistan (UNCIP) had proposed the withdrawal of all Pakistani troops from Pakistan Occupied Kashmir (POK), including those in Gilgit. The British vehemently opposed this proposal because it threatened their entire nuclear monitoring operation. The US State Department was unaware of the clandestine Anglo-US nuclear monitoring operation called Operation Fitzwilliam because this operation violated prevailing US laws and the State Department was not privy to its existence. Such cooperation violated the terms of the McMahon Act of 1946. Therefore, the Americans continued to support a Pakistani withdrawal on the axiom that the Maharaja's accession to India could not be questioned until India lost the proposed plebiscite.

On 4 November 1948, a combat air patrol of two Srinagar-based RIAF Tempest fighters saw an RPAF Dakota on a supply drop over Gilgit and shot it down. Consequently, the Pakistan Cabinet decided that fighter escorts would be provided for future supply drops to Gilgit. Worried Bacon informed his boss Welsh in London. Welsh himself was in turn apprehensive that if this escalated, India might attack Pakistani airfields, notably RAF Chaklala, putting Operation Fitzwilliam into jeopardy.

IMAGE 9.3: Taking a salute (L–R): General Sir Francis Roy Bucher and Air Marshal Thomas W. Elmhirst, IAF. Source: Wikipedia

Pendred at the Joint Photographic Air Intelligence Board in London called up his predecessor the then RIAF Chief Air Marshal Elmhirst and asked him to intervene. Elmhirst reportedly met Nehru and had an hour-long meeting with him in which he succeeded in convincing him to halt all RIAF interdiction of RPAF supply drops to Gilgit. This meant abandoning the simplest way to cut off Gilgit from the Pakistani mainland during the ongoing winter months. Further, it was tantamount to recognising Pakistan's absolute control of the Gilgit Agency.

The fallout of the Elmhirst-Nehru meeting was felt on the ground as well. In November 1948 itself, Lal 'Bagga' Atal took Kargil and was ready to go up the Astore Road to Gilgit. He had signalled to the Northern Command HQ asking for permission to do so. The permission was never granted.

The besieged garrison of Poonch was relieved on 23 November 1948, a full year after its siege, and a firm grip was established by the Indian Army on some of the major portions of the state. Since British national and strategic interests had pre-eminence over those of Pakistan, a ceasefire was now the only honourable and realistic proposition left on the table for both Britain and Pakistan. In fact, Gracey had articulated his fears about India threatening the Jhelum Bridge and the importance of holding the Indian Army to the Uri-Poonch-Naushera line.

Gracey had then conceived of Operation Venus. This operation was a thrust against the Indian line of communication up to the Poonch Valley with infantry and a heavy tank brigade in the Naushera-Beri Patan area. At this stage, the Indian Army was involved in the relief of Poonch and Leh. Operation Venus was executed under Tottenham, who commanded the 7th Division of the Pakistan Army. It was one of Pakistan's two field divisions and was based in Rawalpindi.

Operation Venus was launched on 14 December 1948. The Pakistani attack force for Operation Venus consisted of about six infantry battalions and two armoured regiments. To oppose this, the Indians had two infantry brigades (50 Para Brigade and 80 Infantry Brigade). There were also two armoured regiments—Central India Horse and the Deccan Horse—in the same area. In addition, the Indians also possessed more than 10 armoured regiments outside Kashmir—in Punjab or Western UP—that could move to Kashmir if required.

Unfortunately for him, Tottenham failed to sever the Indian line of communication to Poonch. However, it succeeded in providing support to the argument propounded by a variety of British officers serving in the Indian Army that India was now critically low on ammunition and supplies and would find it difficult to defend its existing positions, let alone undertake ambitious offensive operations. It succeeded in convincing Nehru for a ceasefire, which he accepted.

IMAGE 9.4: (L–R) C. Rajagopalachari and Defence Minister Baldev Singh. Source: Wikipedia

Instrumental in influencing Nehru's mind on the ceasefire was the then British High Commissioner in New Delhi Lieutenant General Sir Archibald Nye. Nye was well known to both Nehru and C. Rajagopalachari, properly known as Rajaji, as he was the first post-Independence Governor of Madras until 7 September 1948. Thereafter, he was directly appointed as British High Commissioner to India. Nye was also Colonel-in-Chief of the Madras Regiment from 10 August 1946 till 31 March 1949. From an Indian point of view, he had impeccable credentials and was believed to be pro-India. Nye met Nehru on 22 November 1948 and was able to convince him of the virtues of a ceasefire.

So, in November 1948, two key British officials, Elmhirst and Nye, weighed in on Nehru to accept the logic of a ceasefire. Earlier in the last week of October, Nehru had spent four days relaxing in the Mountbatten country seat of Broadlands in Hampshire. Since Mountbatten was busy with other matters in London, he left Nehru alone with Edwina Mountbatten. Edwina was to work on Nehru to accept a ceasefire in Kashmir.

However, Nehru was fed up with the state of affairs and announced the replacement of Bucher by Cariappa, the first Indian General of the Indian Army. Bucher worked hard to secure a ceasefire on 1 January 1949, a mere 15 days before he relinquished his office. He and his accomplice in Pakistan, Gracey, thwarted the Indian Army's ambitions of recapturing all of Jammu and Kashmir. The entire war was a mockery that enabled Pakistan to hold on to the Muzaffarabad-Poonch belt and the Gilgit Agency, purely as a result of British perfidy.

It appears that wittingly or unwittingly, Nehru was a part of the plot to restrain the Indian Army from recovering the entire Muzaffarabad-Poonch belt and the Gilgit Agency. Legendary journalist Kuldip Nayar asked Kulwant Singh why he restrained the Indian Army from recovering these territories. Singh replied that he had been told by Nehru to halt the Indian Army's advance at a place where the Kashmiri language was no longer spoken. The logic was that Abdullah's writ extended only to the Kashmiri-speaking areas that were expected to vote for India in the event of a regional plebiscite. This meant that Nehru not only wrote off the recovery of these areas in 1948 but was also prepared for the results of a possible plebiscite in the Indian-held areas of the state as well.

How much did Nehru know or suspect that British intransigence was a consequence of their participation in Operation Fitzwilliam?

Unveiling the deceit

The initiation of the process of independence of India from British rule, which was the granting of Dominion status to both India and Pakistan on 15 August 1947 under the Indian Independence Act, 1947, passed by the British Parliament a month earlier, took place in the backdrop of the tumultuous events in Sinkiang and Britain's concerted attempts to develop a nuclear deterrent to the perceived Soviet nuclear threat. The British acquiesced to the reality of surrendering their 'jewel in the crown' because they no longer had faith in the Indian Army's loyalty to the British Crown. Paradoxically, to pursue their secret agenda of acquiring an independent nuclear deterrence, they needed physical and juridical control over Kashmir and NWFP. Therefore, they proceeded to take steps to unilaterally sequester the then 'independent' state of Jammu and Kashmir from this 'jewel'.

The first step in this process was to convince the nascent political leadership of independent India to defer or pass on the signing of the standstill agreement with Jammu and Kashmir, even though the new Dominion of Pakistan had signed it. This legally prevented the continuance of treaties that bound the state of Jammu and Kashmir to British India. These treaties, particularly the Treaty of Amritsar of 1846, provided the Government of India the legal right to exercise quasi-paramountcy over the state and to immediately send military forces for its aid if needed. By not signing the standstill agreement, the Indian government put itself in a straitjacket and could not legally interfere in Kashmir. This protected the British plan to invade the state by proxy to sustain its military interest's post-Partition.

The second step was to have Mountbatten, the then head of the Dominion of India under the British Crown, introduce a rider or proviso of the 'plebiscite' in his acceptance of the Instrument of Accession signed by Maharaja Hari Singh. This rider was introduced even though it was contrary to the provisions of the Indian Independence Act, 1947. The concepts of morality, plurality and equity were propounded by Mountbatten to justify this inclusion. Funnily enough, these concepts were not supposed to apply to British interests and actions in invading the state through its *kabaili* proxies. This was followed by the political endorsement of this as the 'party line' by Prime Minister Nehru in his radio broadcast on 2 November 1947. The rider of voluntary plebiscite institutionalised the uncertainty in the state's accession to India.

Third, the voluntary restraint placed on the Indian Army by Mountbatten and his complicit British Generals to stop the recovery of the occupied territory of the state at the point where the Kashmiri language ceased to be the lingua franca effectively partitioned the state permanently on the ground by 'metes and bounds', notwithstanding all the political noise made thereafter. This latter fact protected the British seismic and acoustic monitoring stations in the Gilgit Agency to remain under British legal control despite the state's accession to the Dominion of India. This permitted Britain to pursue its political and strategic quest to become an independent nuclear power, which had been denied to it by the US.

Mountbatten's hold over the government of the Dominion of India was so vice-like that from the beginning of the armed invasion of Jammu and Kashmir on 22 October 1947 to the declaration of the ceasefire on 1 January 1949, he consistently managed to dissuade both Nehru and Patel from taking any military steps that would force Pakistan to vacate the areas of the state it had usurped.

It is my calculated assessment that Prime Minister Nehru was wedged between a rock and a hard place by Lord Mountbatten or some other agents of the British

Crown: either halt the Indian Army's advance into the Gilgit Agency and accept the de facto partition of the state of Jammu and Kashmir or retake the Gilgit Agency but enter into a political and military alliance with the British Crown that would permit the British government to continue to operate its own military facilities in India for as long as they chose to do so.

Nehru prevailed upon Home Minister Sardar Patel to give his consent to the first choice. In my considered opinion, this was so because Nehru wanted to cut India's overt 'political ties' with Britain (although he picked Mountbatten to be part of the decision-making process of the post-Partition Cabinet) and to pursue his dream of non-alignment. For Patel, in my view, the perception of the security challenges facing post-Partition India coincided with the perception of the security challenges facing British India. There was no difference as India had inherited the mantle of power from the British Raj, notwithstanding the creation of the Dominion of Pakistan and its sequestration from the body of India.

The Department of External Affairs of the Dominion of India sent a memorandum to British Prime Minister Attlee on 25 October 1947. This memorandum made clear that the real goal of the military intervention by the Indian Army, which was scheduled to begin on 27 October 1947, was not to gain control of the Kashmir Valley but the Gilgit Agency. This memorandum made it clear that the entire state of Jammu and Kashmir was the symbol of India's status as the true successor to the British Raj. It implied that the Dominion of India's strategic interests coincided with those of the British Raj. The arrival of this naïve memorandum on Attlee's desk set the cat among the pigeons, so to speak. It became imperative for the British to use every trick in the magician's book to convincingly thwart this goal so lucidly articulated by the Government of India. What this memorandum failed to fathom was that the political objectives of Prime Minister Nehru were no longer in sync with His Majesty's government's, therefore, the objectives articulated by the memorandum were no longer the objectives of the latter. With the Raj gone, the British in India took on a new avatar, because of which it could no longer participate in the game as partners, but as opponents.

The need for negotiation for a ceasefire in Jammu and Kashmir gained currency with the Templer Report. The fear of the Pakistan Army imploding intensified the pressure on the need for the ceasefire. Their dream of a complete takeover of the state through proxy forces from Pakistan now lay in tatters. The ceasefire brokered by Bucher and Gracey was accepted by both countries and finally came into effect on 1 January 1949. The terms of the ceasefire, as laid out in a UN resolution of 13 August 1948, were adopted by the UN on 5 January 1949. This required Pakistan to withdraw all its forces from the entire state, including the Poonch-Muzaffarabad belt and the Gilgit Agency, while allowing India to maintain minimal military strength to preserve law and order. In full compliance with these conditions, a plebiscite was to be held to determine the future of the state.

The Americans backed the UN plan because they wanted a democratic India with whom they wished to engage in a strategic partnership. The legality of the Instrument of Accession and Indian sovereignty over

Kashmir was never in dispute for the US. Therefore, neither was it willing to endorse the presence of the Pakistani Army in the state nor was it keen on a UN intervention. However, the vital role that the British were playing in monitoring the Soviet nuclear progression under the aegis of Operation Fitzwilliam was used by British Foreign Secretary Bevin to pressurise US Secretary of State George Marshall to water down the strong US stand in favour of India and to obliquely support Pakistan, which was merely a proxy for British policy.

To Pakistan, the plebiscite and these conditions were a shattering blow. It was a considerable gamble for the British and the Pakistanis. Had Pakistan lost, not only would have Azad Kashmir disappeared into Abdullah's empire, but India would have done everything in its power to displace Pakistan from the Gilgit Agency and to regain control over the entire northern frontier. However, right from the outset, both sides converged on one important point—the unity of the state of Jammu and Kashmir. There was no question of holding separate plebiscites in the discordant regions of the state that was once united into a single polity by Gulab Singh and his successors under the Dogra rule.

Chapter 10

The Manifestation of Joe-1

Joe-1

Chelyabinsk is a city in southern Russia, east of the Ural Mountains by the banks of the Miass River. Its origin dates back to the Sintashta culture from the time of the *Rig Veda*. The Soviet dictator Josef Stalin selected Chelyabinsk as the site for a plutonium production plant Combine817. The size of the construction effort was enormous as some 45,000 people worked at the site. In November 1947, NKVD General Boris Muzrokov was appointed the Director of Combine817. Beria regularly visited the site. After many false starts, the reactor successfully became critical by the end of March 1949. Super pure metallic plutonium was needed for nuclear weapons, and the first piece of metallic plutonium was produced at Combine817 on 4 April 1949. Further, Plant V in Combine817 produced the plutonium hemispheres used in the first Soviet bomb named Joe-1 by the Americans and RSD-1 by the Soviets.

By January 1949, all design problems for Joe-1 had been solved. A vast programme of testing started, which lasted till August 1949. The actual test site was 170 kilometres west of Semipalatinsk. The location was a waterless plain about 20 kilometres in diameter and surrounded by low mountains. A 37-metre metal tower was built to place the charge. On 26 August 1949, Beria came to the site. By that time the actual bomb and a backup had been assembled at KB-11. The final assembly of the device was completed at 3:00 AM on 29 August 1949, and the device was placed in the 37-metre tower. By 6:00 AM, all preparations were completed. At 7:00 AM on 29 August 1949, the Soviet plutonium bomb copied from the American trinity design was detonated. It was a fabulous success.

The impact

Local time in Gilgit is GMT+5, whereas in Semipalatinsk it is GMT+6. At 6:07 AM Pakistan Standard Time (PST) on 29 August 1949, the impact of the first surface wave from Semipalatinsk was recorded at Station Stowage in the Gilgit Agency. Professor Thirlway rushed in his dressing gown and striped pyjamas to the laboratory vault, 50 yards away from his quarters, after being awoken by his Pakistani servant. What he read off the seismograph was tremendous. If an underground earthquake had occurred at Semipalatinsk, then its intensity exceeded 15,000 tons of Trinitrotoluene (TNT). An excited Thirlway immediately dictated an urgent message to Welsh in London, which was dispatched by encrypted signal at around 6:30 AM PST and was received in London at TAL's Shell-Mex House office on the Strand at 1:30 AM GMT. The Duty Officer rang Welsh on a secure line and sent him a typed copy of the decrypted message by motorcycle.

On reading the message, Welsh woke up C. The latter in turn called up Attlee at 10 Downing Street. A sleepy Attlee asked C to come over and bring Welsh with him. Meanwhile, Welsh sent a code red message to his counterpart at the Joint Air Photographic Intelligence Board to scramble a flight of Lincoln bombers from RAF Chaklala in Rawalpindi. The flight of five Lincoln bombers was to collect nuclear debris in an area covering an arc from Khojand in Soviet Tajikistan to Urumqi in Sinkiang. By 7:15 AM PST, the Lincoln bombers fitted with air sampling filters were winging their way towards the Soviet Union. This first flight of Lincolns had orders to fly regular search paths.

A second flight of five Lincolns took off from RAF Chaklala at 9:15 AM PST, exactly two hours after the first flight. These aircraft were supported by a flight of five Halifax aircraft piloted by the Poles. Another flight of Polish-flown Halifax aircraft from Risalpur took to the skies. These aircraft were all following a backtracked trajectory of the air carrying the radioactivity. In such cases, if the radioactive debris can also be dated, the approximate location of the explosion can be determined. Back-to-back sorties by Lincoln and Halifax aircraft were flown over 48 hours from the first take-off to collect an extraordinary amount of data to validate the manifestation of Joe-1.

The meeting that Attlee had with C and Welsh concluded with the decision that all means were to be used to scientifically conclude beyond reasonable doubt that a Soviet bomb had been detonated that morning in Semipalatinsk. Only then would they share this information with the Americans. Further, the British could not take any public credit for this discovery because it would result in pulling out all the Kashmir skeletons from the closet and making them public.

Validating the evidence

British nuclear scientists in the 1940s knew that in the period immediately following detonation, the energy generated by a nuclear explosion appears primarily in the form of thermal radiation. This radiation diffuses out from the exploding device and into the surrounding air, heating up the air and forming an isothermal sphere. For a 15-kiloton explosion, like Joe-1, a shockwave forms when the sphere has a radius of about 10 miles, which occurs at about 0.2 milliseconds after the explosion. Shortly after this time, hydrodynamic effects dominate and the shockwave propagation becomes independent of the source mechanism. As the shockwave moves outward, its strength and speed decrease. Eventually, the shockwave degenerates into an acoustic wave.

In the real atmosphere, homogeneities strongly affect the propagation of the acoustic signal. The most important homogeneity is the variation of the sound speed with altitude. The temperature of the atmosphere decreases from sea level to about 10 kilometres altitude, remains constant between 10 and 30 kilometres and then increases. Since the speed of sound is proportional to the square root of the temperature of the atmosphere, higher altitudes form a low-velocity waveguide for sonic propagation. The acoustic signals from explosions propagate to great distances principally in this waveguide. The principal periods in the acoustic signal are from about one-half seconds to several minutes.

Since background acoustic noise is rarely greater than five dynes per square centimetre, a one-kiloton explosion can, with high probability, be detected up to distances of about 1,400 kilometres. Joe-1 was a 15-kiloton blast. To locate an acoustic source, at least three signals at widely separated points must be detected. However, as per available records in the public domain, the British only operated two acoustic stations in the Gilgit Agency, namely Beaver and Tagday. Logically speaking, there must have been a third acoustic station. Circumstantial evidence points to this acoustic station being located in the village of Raskam in the Shaksgam Valley, which Pakistan turned over to China in 1963 along with the remnants of the acoustic station. The other alternative to consider is that Stowage also had an acoustic monitoring facility. In the absence of declassified information, one can only speculate about the configuration and number of acoustic monitoring stations.

Because of the presence of the earth's ionosphere, the electromagnetic field propagates to great distances dispersively with cylindrical divergence. In the case of an explosion at altitudes about one kilometre, the asymmetry produced by the ground is no longer present. The remaining asymmetries are less than the ground asymmetry and, consequently, the radiated signal is expected to have reduced amplitude. Above a few kilometres, the asymmetry caused by the variation in atmospheric density is expected to become increasingly important and the signal magnitude is expected to increase. Under ordinary circumstances, the electromagnetic signal can be detected at distances of many thousands of kilometres. While acoustic and radio signals provide a sensitive means of detecting nuclear explosions, similar signals are generated by natural events. Only the collection of radioactive debris constitutes positive identification of nuclear explosions. Shortly after the explosion, the fission products that remain in the troposphere are confined to a relatively small volume of air. With time, the volume of air containing the fission products increases because of tropospheric winds, and depending upon the wind patterns, it moves to great distances.

All the British stations in the Gilgit Agency also collected the nuclear debris as aforementioned, once it had descended back to earth. These three stations were already collecting four filters' worth of material a day that was being flown from Chaklala airbase in Rawalpindi directly to RAF Harwell in Oxfordshire, UK, for radiochemical analysis by Dr Morgan's team as described earlier. The significance of these activities is not that they happened but the closeness of the Soviet test site in Semipalatinsk to British bases in the Gilgit Agency.

Finally, cryptanalysts at the SIGINT station in Abbottabad were poring over, translating and decrypting all Soviet radio traffic within and from Central Asia to Northern Russia.

How the Soviets knew that the British monitored Joe-1 from Gilgit

In June 1949, Mao Tse-tung, Chairman of the CPC, dispatched a delegation to Moscow headed by Liu Shao-chi. Liu was the Vice-Chairman of the Central People's Government in China's regions that were newly liberated from the KMT. Liu's mandate was to ascertain the Soviet position regarding the imminent victory of the CPC in China proper. Stalin, who was anxiously pressurising his nuclear scientists to conduct a test to detonate the first Soviet nuclear bomb, advised the Chinese delegation to accelerate their liberation of Sinkiang. Stalin was anxious to secure and monopolise the access to Sinkiang's uranium, thorium, beryllium and molybdenum mines.

IMAGE 10.1: (L–R) Soviet dictator Joseph Stalin, President Harry S. Truman and Prime Minister Winston Churchill. Source: Public Domain

Stalin warned Liu of a US and British 'plot' to encourage the 'Five Mas', a clique of five Muslim warlords—Ma Pu-fang, Ma Zhongying, Ma Hongkui, Ma Lin and Ma Hu-shan—all owing their allegiance to the KMT government in Nanking to retreat to Sinkiang and establish an independent Muslim State. This claim had some basis, with the US Consul in Tihwa John Paxton requesting Washington's guidance regarding the possibility of supplying Ma Pu-fang with material aid if he retreated to Sinkiang. This information came to Stalin via Kim Philby, MI6 Liaison Officer with US intelligence agencies in Washington DC. Philby was also a Soviet spy. Despite the existence of the top-secret TAL within MI6 and Welsh's tight control over the release of any information about nuclear matters, the fact is that all MI6 communications to the Americans via Philby were known to the Soviets.

IMAGE 10.2: Kim Philby, a double agent with MI6 and KGB.
Source: Wikipedia

Philby also reported to his KGB masters that US Secretary of State Dean Acheson was flying to New Delhi in July 1949 to do the groundwork for Nehru's visit to the US in October later that year. This information sent Stalin into a tizzy. First, he instructed the Soviet Charge d'affaires in Teheran to convey to the Pakistani Ambassador in Teheran, Raja Ghazanfar Ali Khan, Stalin's invitation to the Pakistani Prime Minister, Liaquat Ali Khan, to visit Moscow. This invitation was extended orally on 2 June 1949. Second, he ordered the KGB chief Lavrenti Beria to rapidly launch a disinformation campaign to sabotage any possible chance of India formally joining the Western Alliance. In a classic exercise in disinformation, the Soviet news agency TASS, in a report dated 6 July 1949, openly warned the world about Anglo-American aggression against the USSR through Gilgit.

What was this aggression that the report referred to? It was the British acoustic and seismic monitoring stations in the Gilgit Agency, which the Soviets wanted shutting before their forthcoming nuclear test in Semipalatinsk on 29 August 1949. The TASS report also highlighted the suppression of communists in Pakistan and spoke favourably at length about the anti-feudal Abdullah and his petty-bourgeois overlord in New Delhi Prime Minister Nehru.

On 29 July 1949, while in New Delhi, the US Secretary of State Dean Acheson ordered the US Consulate in Tihwa to be closed. Deputy Counsel Douglas Mackiernan was ordered to stay behind, officially to destroy consular records and equipment but covertly to continue atomic intelligence activities.

This information was shared with MI6 through Philby and also divulged to the NKVD.

During his stay in New Delhi, Acheson signed a secret protocol with Bhola Nath Mullick, India's IB chief. The protocol involved intelligence sharing between India and the US on China. This information was also leaked to the Soviets via Philby.

On 10 August 1949, Mackiernan sent another classified and encrypted message to Acheson, who was still in New Delhi, acknowledging his continued and sustained operation of the long-range atomic explosion detection equipment until the imminent Soviet test took place.

The British, worried that the Soviets might compromise Liaquat Ali Khan and thus place their bases in the Gilgit Agency in jeopardy, piled in heavily and had Khan's scheduled visit to Moscow on 17 August 1949 scrapped.

Stalin fumed when he received feedback from Philby that he had been thwarted by the British. Philby also tipped off Moscow after the British confirmation of Joe-1 was sent to his superior, Wilfred Mann, the MI6 Resident in Washington DC on 2 September 1949. The Americans had to independently confirm this fact and also release this news to the world as if it had been a unique American discovery. On 3 September 1949, a USAF B-29 collected radioactive samples over the northern Pacific. A further B-29 flight on 5 September 1949 collected additional samples over Japan. Detailed analysis was undertaken by Tracerlab Inc., the Department of Defence contractor. They found that the samples collected were artificial and had been injected into the atmosphere by an artificial occurrence. Thereafter, an elaborate charade was constructed whereby the British were informed on 10 September 1949 by a top-secret telex conference of the same event they had so ingenuously and laboriously detected themselves. This Anglo-US collaborative exercise, as mentioned earlier, went by the code name Operation Fitzwilliam and had been in operation since early 1948.

Right after the detonation of Joe-1, an ad hoc committee was set up in the US by Admiral Roscoe Hillenkoetter, Director of Central Intelligence Agency, that concluded that Operation Fitzwilliam had more successes than failures. The USAF was instructed thereafter to expand its detection capability and base it on even more intensive collaboration with the British. This meant that the importance of the three/four British detection stations in the Gilgit Agency and the exhaustive usage of Chaklala and Risalpur airbases by the RAF would only gain in importance. This in turn would necessitate consolidating on the ground the advantages that Pakistan made from the UN-mandated ceasefire put in place on 1 January 1949. For India, it meant that the Kashmir problem would never be resolved. There would never be a plebiscite as Pakistani troops would never withdraw from the positions they had occupied on the ground as a result of the events post-24 October 1947. They were under British control, and what had been seized would be retained not vacated. This was the same policy that the East India Company had employed since 1757 and the British carried forward 192 years later. Nothing had changed.

Stalin moves to secure his nuclear essentials

Meanwhile, in Moscow, Stalin also suggested that CCP make use of the East Turkestan Republic in Sinkiang and establish communications with them. Consequently, Deng Li-qun, Political Secretary in Liu's delegation, was dispatched from Moscow to Ili in East Turkestan with a radio communications team to establish contact between the East Turkestan Republic's leadership and the CCP's.

Li-qun arrived in Ili on 14 August 1949 to begin the task of establishing links with the East Turkestan Republic's leadership. To this end, Li-qun met with their major leaders, Ahmetjan, Ishaq Beg and Abbasoff, three days later. Apparently, at this meeting, Li-qun presented the three leaders with a letter from Mao that praised the East Turkestan Republic and acclaimed their rebellion as being part of China's 'democratic revolutionary movement'. Significantly, Li-qun also invited them to send a delegation to the inaugural Chinese People's Political Consultative Conference (CPPCC) that was scheduled for 21 September 1949 in Peking, which had been newly 'liberated' from the KMT by the CCP. Subsequently, a delegation comprising Ahmetjan, Ishaq Beg and Abbasoff and complemented by a representative of the KMT-held region in Sinkiang, Luo Zhi, left via the Soviet Union for Peking. However, they never made it to Peking. Their plane crashed somewhere in the Soviet Union around 27 August 1949.

Two days later, Joe-1 was detonated on 29 August 1949 in Semipalatinsk.

To rapidly ramp up testing and start serial production of nuclear bombs, Stalin needed to secure adequate supplies of his nuclear materials from within his backyard.

Mao had practically won the civil war in China. Stalin was wary of Mao using the US card as a counter to the Soviet Union. He never wanted a US presence on China's borders with the Soviets. He, therefore, agreed to provide air transport to the People's Liberation Army (PLA) troops to be rapidly flown into Tihwa. Almost 14,000 PLA troops under Peng Dehuai's command in north-west China were flown into Tihwa early in October 1949. These developments led to the surrender of both the KMT civilian and military authorities even before any PLA troops entered Sinkiang by land.

Stalin thus made two deft moves. First, as has been described, he sent an air armada of over 40 transport aircraft to fly PLA troops to Tihwa. Second, he encouraged the leadership of the East Turkestan Republic to establish contact with the CPC and merge three districts of the East Turkestan Republic into a CPC-controlled Sinkiang. This effectively ring-fenced Sinkiang into the Soviet orbit.

Events outmanoeuvre Nehru

In the autumn of 1949, India and Nehru faced some very critical choices. For Nehru, it was yet another predicament like the one he faced in 1947. By choosing the wrong option in 1947, he had lost a third of the state of Jammu and Kashmir to Pakistan. He was blissfully unaware that by opting to be neutral in the Cold War he stood to lose another fifth of the state to China in the following months. Nehru's grand obsession to lead the entire decolonising Third World made him wear rose-tinted glasses while looking at the Soviet bloc. One wonders how he could have been so naïve as to be unaware that he was poised to expose India to institutionalised uncertainty along her borders for decades, if not centuries, to come if he chose wrongly yet again. The choice before Nehru was to remain a marginal self-deluded 'neutral' player who would be pushed around by the Soviet bloc as an inconsequential 'also ran' or to boldly join the US and the UK as the bulwark and frontline State of the free world against communism. There was no other choice.

Nehru possibly wanted to emulate Mahatma Gandhi who went down in the annals of history as the originator of a unique universal philosophy. Gandhi was the patron saint of non-violence, and he cemented his place in history despite an attempt by Subhas Chandra Bose to overreach him and throw the independence movement into armed conflict. Nehru wanted to be remembered in history as the patron saint of non-alignment. He overruled his bête noire Sardar Patel whose natural inclination was to join the Western Alliance. But in choosing to remain neutral, Nehru compromised the future of the nascent Indian Republic.

A wary Stalin ring-fences Mao

Stalin needed Sinkiang's vast cache of atomic minerals to transition to serial production of bombs.

These minerals would need to be transported to Combine6 in Khojand. Further, he did not want Soviet forces to fight the Muslim secessionists like Osman Bator. Stalin wanted a proxy force to battle the insurgents and enable Soviet technicians to get at the ore. The Soviets were tired of battling the Muslim insurgents. Stalin's main reason why the Soviet Union maintained Sinkiang as a Chinese territory rather than creating an independent State as they had done with Outer Mongolia was because he feared that once a Muslim State was established in Sinkiang, the Muslims of other Soviet Central Asian Republics would also demand independence. Furthermore, an independent Muslim State would be hard to control because the independence-seeking Ili clique had already caused a great deal of trouble for Moscow.

IMAGE 10.3: Mao Tse-tung and Joseph Stalin with others in Moscow, December 1949. Source: Wikimedia Commons

Therefore, his moves in Sinkiang were very much in line with his general distrust of Mao. This became apparent when Mao visited Moscow in December 1949. This was Mao's first-ever foreign trip. His objective was to seek an alliance with the Soviet Union which would enable him to turn China into a world power. The key was not how many weapons Stalin would provide but what technology and infrastructure would he provide to manufacture armaments in China. It took a good two months before the Sino-Soviet Treaty of Friendship and Mutual Assistance was signed on 14 February 1950 after intense negotiation. Stalin imposed harsh and rigid terms on the Chinese and also comprehensively ring-fenced Mao so that he could never gang up with the Americans against Stalin. Under the terms of the 1950 aid agreements, China was to receive 300 million dollars' worth of military assistance divided equally over five years. Half of the loan was earmarked for the Chinese Navy. The loan was to be repaid by China with exports of raw materials. This effectively tied Chinese extractive industries to Soviet processing facilities and markets. Stalin cleverly deepened China's dependence on the Soviet Union.

But the jewel in the crown was the establishment of the Sino-Soviet Non-Ferrous and Rare Metals Company near Tihwa in Sinkiang on 27 March 1950. Its object was to prospect and mine for radioactive minerals. Soviet domination of this venture resulted in all of the uranium, thorium, molybdenum and beryllium production being appropriated by the USSR. The Sino-Soviet Petroleum Company was also set up in Sinkiang on the same date.

The first task before both of these companies was to undertake an intensive survey of Sinkiang's mineral wealth and updating the geological and resource maps in use in the province to direct operations. Geological operations for the companies focused on the extraction of an assortment of minerals, more specifically beryllium, lithium, as well as niobium and tantalum. Geological expeditions focused their efforts on pinpointing caches of valuable minerals.

The immediate area of interest of these operations was focused in three primary places: the far northern stretches of the Altai Mountains, an area near Kashgar in the far south called the Tarim Basin and Ili along the Soviet border. Indeed, the operations of the geological team from the Sino-Soviet Non-Ferrous and Rare Metals Company appeared to confirm the views held by scholars in the Soviet Academy of Sciences, which concluded that beryllium and lithium ore beds of the company were the largest reserves of minerals in the world. Since neither Sinkiang nor China enjoyed the industrial capacity and high technological abilities to use the rare earth minerals, all of them that were produced at various sites were shipped directly to the Soviet Union.

It is important to point out that in both geological and territorial terms, the Tarim Basin consisted of the entire catchment area of the basin, including the entire Karakash River right from its source in India. The Tarim Basin emerged in 1950 as a critical mineral and political resource for both the Soviets and the Chinese. An unpublished report from 1950, written by the Soviet Ministry of Oil for the Sino-Soviet Oil Company, and which is contained in China's Central Geological Survey, noted that of the three regions to be targeted for oil exploration, the most important one was in the Kashgar region of Sinkiang in the far southern stretches of the province deep in the Tarim Basin. To help uncover these oil resources, the report called for the organisation of geological expeditionary teams. These teams would work around the clock during the five months when the weather allowed for geological surveying in Sinkiang. The Soviets had an ambitious plan that had precise goals with little room for error. The objective was to complete an exhaustive survey of the province's oil wealth by the end of 1955.

Likewise, the geological planning reports called for 7 of the proposed 41 expeditionary teams to be focused on the Tarim Basin. Hidden in fine print in the reports, the Tarim Basin was viewed as a single consolidated geographical entity. The fact that different political boundaries transcended this geographical entity was cleverly ignored and suppressed. The adage 'finders keepers, losers weepers' was the prevailing mantra.

Stalin had had his way, but the unification of China under the rule of the communist party also paved the way for the creation of a potential rival within the communist bloc. Further, since several thousand Soviet geologists, hydrologists, mining engineers, atomic scientists and security officials were to be now officially based in Sinkiang, a separate agreement was signed concerning the working conditions of Soviet specialists in Sinkiang. Another agreement signed on 25 October 1950 offered technical assistance for the installation and operation of Soviet equipment. Chinese assistants were assigned to Soviet scientists in Sinkiang, where nuclear test reactors were reported in 1951.

During his conversations with Mao, Stalin emphatically praised the communist party's control of Sinkiang. Stalin was a ruthless 20th-century pioneer of ethnopolitics, who prodded Mao to increase the percentage of Han Chinese residents in Sinkiang to 30 per cent from a low of 5 per cent, to reduce the overwhelming Muslim majority, strengthen border security and oppose British intrigues in Sinkiang. Stalin argued that by being continually present in the Pakistan Army, the British had enough capability to immediately activate Muslims across the border in the Gilgit Agency to fight the civil war, clearly undesirable, in Sinkiang against the communist party. Stalin cleverly concealed the existence of the British nuclear monitoring stations in the Gilgit Agency from Mao. Instead, he told Mao that Sinkiang had large deposits of oil and extensive cotton cultivation and that China needed these badly. Since Stalin did not trust Mao, he deliberately underplayed the reliance on Sinkiang's uranium, thorium, beryllium and molybdenum deposits by the Soviet nuclear programme. In fact, the Soviet side slipped in their need for exclusive access to these atomic minerals only on 27 March 1950 when the subsidiary agreements were being executed long after Mao and his close advisers left Moscow for Peking. The essence of the treaty was in these secret annexes.

The signing of the treaty also publicly indicated to the world that both the Soviets and China were now economically and militarily aligned in a tight embrace.

It did not require rocket science to infer that all of communist China's strategic and political moves in Asia had the endorsement of Moscow. China was the client State of the Soviet Union. This development did not augur well for Tibet and India. Added to this was the attitude of Stalin towards India. Stalin famously referred to the transfer of power by the British on 15 August 1947 as a 'political farce', and a few months later refused to send condolences on the death of Mahatma Gandhi. While Stalin considered Nehru to be an agent of American imperialism, Soviet Foreign Minister Vyacheslav Molotov considered Nehru to be a British intelligence agent.

Soviet military circles reasoned that in the event of a war with the US, India being a member of the British Commonwealth would inevitably act as an enemy of the USSR, and the Indian airfields and other military-strategic facilities would be used for bombing raids along the southern borders of the Soviet Union. *Pravda*, a Soviet communist party newspaper, wrote on 10 August 1947 that out of 19 English Major Generals 16 remained in India, and out of 280 Brigadier Generals, 260 would remain in India in support of the idea that India must retain military and political allegiance with its former mother country. A view was taken that one of the reasons the Sino-Soviet alignment cemented was precisely to counter such an outcome.

Stalin prods Mao to move into Tibet and Aksai Chin

Stalin had two supplementary objectives. The first was to build a road connecting Pulu in Sinkiang to Gartok in Tibet. This road would cut through Aksai Chin, enabling Soviet technicians, engineers and geologists to access the mineral deposits and transport the excavated minerals to Khojand by road. Second, to further eliminate the limited presence of the northernmost Indian military escort in Gartok, Tibet, at the Indo-Tibet trade mart, Stalin urged Mao to consolidate Chinese control in north-western Tibet bordering Sinkiang. He ordered Mao not to delay in sending troops from Sinkiang to keep a watch on the hostile lamas who, he alleged, were willing to sell it to the highest bidder, be it America, Britain or India. Because of the British monitoring stations in the Gilgit Agency, Stalin feared that the British officers still serving in the Indian Army would use these troops in Tibet for espionage or to beef up their strength to conduct special operations against the Soviet sites in Sinkiang. Neither the British nor the new Indian government was aware that Soviet geologists had discovered significant deposits of uranium, thorium, beryllium and molybdenum ores in the Tarim Basin in southern Sinkiang that bordered Aksai Chin. The location of these deposits extended into the Karakash River valley in Aksai Chin. Stalin wanted to ensure that only he had access to these deposits and not the British or the Americans. Therefore, what better way to secure these deposits than by using the Chinese as mules to extract the ores and lug them to the roadheads that would transport them to Khojand?

IMAGE 10.4: Major S.M. Krishnatry (centre), Commander of Indian Military Escort in Tibet, 1947–1954. Source: AIM Television Archives

Western Tibet was thousands of miles away from Lhasa, the seat of the Tibetan government. Gaining control of western Tibet was only symbolic. For Mao, this symbolism was enough to wage a propaganda war over the rest of Tibet, by using western Tibet as a base. Mao also realised that because Tibet did not have a network of roads, the logistics of supporting an invasion would be extremely challenging. Further, this would necessarily limit the size of his invasion force. So, on 22 January 1950 when Stalin prodded him to accelerate the invasion of western Tibet, Mao extracted a Soviet commitment to airdrop supplies to the Chinese invasion force in Tibet. Further, the Tibetan Army was tough and gritty and prepared to give a plucky fight to the PLA. Therefore, Mao decided it was better for him to play Stalin's game till the PLA was fully prepared for the invasion of eastern and central Tibet.

Symbolically, in the meantime, the PLA marched into some parts of eastern Tibet that were easily accessible and did not offer any resistance. They circulated a 10-point document asking Tibetans to cooperate with China in 'liberating' Tibet from foreign imperialists. Since 90 per cent of the 'imperialists' in Tibet were the Indian trade officials and their Indian Army escorts in Gartok, Yatung and Lhasa, it did not require knowledge of rocket science to understand who the PLA was referring to.

Chapter 11

The Soviet-Inspired Chinese Invasion of Aksai Chin

On Stalin's orders, Mao dispatches the PLA to Khotan

During their discussions in Moscow in December 1949, Stalin ordered Mao to immediately start the construction of the Sinkiang-Tibet road through what was perceived to be Indian Territory. This became a top priority and, as a consequence, orders to this effect were issued by Mao from Moscow in December 1949 itself. For Stalin, the tentative discovery of uranium ores in and around the valley of the Karakash River in Aksai Chin was a godsend. Kurchatov's F-1 nuclear reactor in the Soviet Union was not as efficient as Enrico Fermi's reactor in the US. It needed almost eight times more uranium per weapon. Therefore, to create a stockpile of nuclear weapons for the Soviet strategic forces, rapid action was needed to discover and extract uranium ores. The supply chain of ores from northern Sinkiang needed to be augmented. Though the presence of these ores had been established in Aksai Chin via aerial surveys, extracting them and transporting them through the treacherous heights of the Himalayas, Karakoram and Pamirs was a formidable challenge for Soviet technology. The ores had to be transported to

Khojand in Tajikistan. This could not happen without a road network.

Secrecy and urgency were of paramount importance. The British presence in the Gilgit Agency and how it had been established and then re-secured after the Partition of India convinced Stalin that the minute the British got a whiff of the presence of uranium ores in Aksai Chin, they would take immediate steps to both secure the source and deny it to the Soviets. They would also then bring in the Americans and make the test site at Semipalatinsk extremely vulnerable to attack. Further, the set-up at Khojand would also become more vulnerable to possible attack. Paranoia fed paranoia. Stalin had to create his nuclear stockpile yesterday!

The vital road would enable PLA soldiers to easily drive down from Sinkiang to Gartok and keep a close watch on the activities of the Indian military escort permanently stationed there since 1904. Stalin was paranoid that with Gartok easily accessible through the caravan route from Ladakh, these troops could very easily be augmented by road and by dropping paratroops by air. Therefore, it was very important to install actual PLA markers in Tibet.

Did Prime Minister Nehru never discover this aspect of Sino-Soviet perfidy? Why didn't Nehru's sister, Vijaylakshmi Pandit, who was the then India's Ambassador to Moscow, and her successor Dr S. Radhakrishnan report on these far-reaching developments? Didn't Nehru have Captain Ram Sathe as the Indian Consul in Kashgar till January 1950? What feedback did Sathe radio to New Delhi? Was IB chief Mullick not aware of the Sino-Soviet alliance and their interests in Sinkiang? Why are the dispatches sent by Sathe to New Delhi still classified? Why did Nehru abandon India's stance of neutrality in favour of newly born communist China by recognising the communist regime on 30 December 1949 when the evidence pointed to the conspiracy of Stalin and Mao against Nehru?

Author Michael Dillon, surprisingly, answers all these questions in his seminal work *Xinjiang and the Expansion of Chinese Communist Power*. Why doesn't the Government of India set the record straight even today? Isn't it time to let future generations know of Nehru's magnificent obsession with the Chinese and what this folly cost India? Isn't it time to uncover the cloak of institutionalised untruths that have governed India's China policy since independence?

In December 1949, days after the first Stalin-Mao conversation, PLA officer Bai Chushi's unit—the 15th Regiment of the PLA that bivouacked in Aksu north of Kashgar—was given orders to immediately march due south across the Taklamakan Desert, following the Khotan River and taking the city of Khotan (Heitan) some 325 miles east of Kashgar. It took them 17 gruelling days to reach Khotan, which was the centre of the Uyghur Muslim resistance. There was no secrecy about this expedition as arrangements were made by the locals at each night halt to provide food, fodder and water. A local Uyghur called Abdula was their guide through the treacherous Taklamakan Desert. They also had two young Uyghur officers called Mahmud Niyaz and Omar Ruzi from the Soviet side of the East Turkestan Republic; they spoke fluent Mandarin and Turkic and were an invaluable asset to the expedition.

Once they had secured Khotan, fresh orders reached Chushi by radio. He was asked to immediately secure the border posts at the Khunjerab and Mintaka Passes on the Sinkiang-Gilgit Agency border. Chushi immediately sent a message to the KMT border guards that the PLA was shortly arriving to relieve them. The KMT guards all fled to Ladakh via the Gilgit Agency. It is inconceivable that these KMT drifters were not interrogated by the Indian Army's Field Intelligence Unit (FIU) in either Kargil or Ladakh.

The 15th Regiment of PLA entrusted to build a road through Aksai Chin

It is a matter of record that the 15th Regiment had been a part of the 359th Brigade of the PLA during the Second World War. It was based in a mountain gorge at Nanniwan, which is south-east of Yunnan. Nanniwan is where the CCP had its base after the Long March. At Nanniwan, the 15th Regiment was deployed in opening up uncultivated land and in the production of agricultural implements. This was the 'Nanniwan spirit' that showed the mettle of these troops.

Soon after in January 1950, Chushi received orders to depute a battalion of soldiers to open a road through the mountains and assist in the rapid liberation of Tibet. While three companies were left behind in Khotan, two companies plus the machine gun company and the battalion HQ staff were sent into the Kunlun Mountains to construct the Sinkiang-Tibet Highway through Aksai Chin. Thus began the process of trespassing into Indian Territory at Haji Langar and exiting it at the Lanak La Pass.

To beef up the technical expertise of his team, Chushi commissioned the services of a KMT defector Major General Liang Hanwei and some of his engineering colleagues. The team made its way to the foot of the Kunlun range. Hanwei's team of engineers was instrumental in training and supervising the men of the 15th Regiment in surveying and road building. Because Chushi had no topographical maps of the region, he had to rely on information from the communities of local inhabitants to send survey parties into the high peaks in freezing conditions. Moreover, because of the enormous complexity of the task, Chushi received orders on 1 April 1950 to relocate his entire battalion from Khotan to their then-location in the Kunlun Mountains. They were also to be joined by the independent cavalry division of the Sinkiang Military District. The existing force had to be augmented as it was woefully short in numbers, and despite having moved into the relative safety of their mountainous retreat, they were still facing heavy rain, sandstorms, blizzards and freezing temperatures. It was a test of will for the PLA, and this story has become a part of current Chinese national mythology. This was a manifestation of the true 'Nanniwan spirit'.

This comparatively large force set up their base camp on a peak called Pulukazi or simply Pulu. It is inconceivable that such a large force and its activities could remain concealed from locals, travellers, traders and spies. They constantly needed supplies transported by caravans. Word travels fast even in the mountains. What travelled even faster was news of the discovery of gold by the troops in Pulukazi. The party committee permitted the troops to search for gold mines and dig for gold at certain sites, while the advance survey parties completed their work.

The Regimental Commander Jiang Yuhe who stayed back at Khotan came to know of a man called Yuan who was an experienced gold prospector. Yuan was sent to the Pulukazi base camp. He guided the troops to the most promising mines and taught them how to mine as well as pan for gold in the waters of the Karakash River that flowed from within Indian Territory into Sinkiang. Since the river is fed by melting snow, it was dry in winter and spring. It was the only natural dry riverbed passage during those days in the geographical feature called the Tarim Basin. More troops were deployed as a veritable treasure trove of valuable minerals emerged from the riverbed, like gemstones and jade, apart from other minerals that yielded asbestos, rock crystal and jet-black coal. To the officers and commissars of the PLA, it became clear in the first half of 1950 itself that the entire Tarim Basin, including the Karakash River that was the primary source of water to this area, contained very valuable resources over which they wished to retain control. What these officials of the new communist State of China never realised is that they were engaging in international loot and theft. They were actually stealing from the Government of India.

Stalin was equally interested in dominating control over the spoils. As far as the Soviets were concerned, all 'legally' extracted ores and minerals belonged to the Sino-Soviet Non-Ferrous and Rare Metals Company. No concern was given to the fact that there was no legal permission or right for this company to extract minerals and ores from the sovereign Indian Territory. The operating principle was very simple. Since there was no physical presence of any Indian official, simply absorb this territory and start extracting and mining for ores. Therefore, unwittingly from India's point of view, atomic minerals and metals mined from sovereign Indian Territory were flowing to the Soviet Union, which was conveniently using them for its nuclear programme. Was Nehru aware or concerned by this Sino-Soviet intrusion into and theft of valuable resources from Indian Territory?

In fact, the Indian Army escort at Gartok sent radio messages back to New Delhi. I had the occasion to meet retired Major S.M. Krishnatry who commanded the Indian Army escort in Tibet from 1947–1954 when the PLA came into Gartok in June 1951. He said he radioed this information to Army HQ in New Delhi. The reply he received was to sit tight and observe. And that is what we have been doing ever since.

Meanwhile, the much-delayed cavalry division led by Hong Yadong finally arrived in the Kunlun Mountains. The 15th Regiment was placed under his command. That the mission of this augmented force was of vital importance cannot be underscored. Working furiously with climbing ropes, rock hammers and dynamite, the 208.5-kilometre road was completed by May 1951. By the time their work drew to a close, the PLA in Sinkiang had settled down after brutally eliminating all opposition for the time being. The men in Pulukazi were supplied by a double-humped Bactrian camel battalion, and these ferried them food, horse fodder, tents, tools and medicines. The military transport department in Kashgar provided lorries once the road became operational.

The feat of this exercise was not kept hidden. Much publicity was generated to praise this Herculean task. The Central Military Commission in Peking sent a film crew to make a documentary that was shown all over China. The Xinhua News Agency released several stories indicating that troops needed for mopping up operations in Tibet after the invasion would be sent by road across the Kunlun Mountains. Wang Emmao, the Party Secretary of the PLA 2nd Army addressed a conference of CPC delegates in Kashgar in which he showered praise on all the veterans of this road-building exercise. In 1952, the PLA's Southwest Military Region issued a commemorative medal on the liberation of Tibet to all the veterans of this campaign.

The secret of Lop Nor

IMAGE 11.1: Chinese nuclear scientists Qian Sanqiang and He Zehui who located Lop Nor. Source: Wikimedia Commons

The first expeditionary team that drove into the Tarim Basin in March 1950 in a convoy of battered and rusty Willys Jeeps belonging to the former KMT government had an unusually important member on board. This was Qian Sanqiang, a French-trained Chinese nuclear scientist. Unknown to the Soviets and other Chinese assistants provided to them, Sanqiang's superior was Kang Sheng, the head of the Chinese secret service called Tewu. Sheng was also the head of the monitoring group that oversaw China's super-secret Nuclear Council. This latter body was set up in December 1949, just weeks after the formation of the People's Republic of China (PRC) itself.

IMAGE 11.2: Kang Sheng, communist China's first intelligence chief. Source: Wikipedia

Sanqiang's mission was to detect uranium and thorium deposits identified by Soviet aerial reconnaissance and on the ground identify the most suitable options for locating nuclear bases. He zeroed in on the Tarim Basin to a triangle with the three vertices of Lake Lop Nor, the town of Yuli and the Turfan Depression, which is a fault trough. The convoy while travelling through this identified area was frequently attacked by an assortment of Mongol bandits, Uyghur pillagers, Red Army deserters, desert brigands, stray bands of KMT stragglers and legendary Manchu tiger hunters. Despite these perils and injuries that caused Sanqiang to be replaced by his equally competent nuclear scientist wife He Zehui, the conquest of the Tarim Basin proceeded unrelentingly.

Notwithstanding usual Soviet propaganda, there is no question that China's oil and mining industry in Sinkiang should be indebted to the Soviets. Soviet geologists led 19 surveying teams into Sinkiang to survey the province's mineral wealth in the years between 1951 and 1954 and also helped lay the foundation for transportation and infrastructural development. Soviet geologists and surveyors thus played a central role in the day-to-day surveying and geological operations of the two entities. Of the 262-person staff of the geological office in the Sino-Soviet Oil Company in 1954, 30 per cent were so-called Soviet 'experts'. An additional 348 Soviet experts worked in the Sino-Soviet Non-Ferrous and Rare Metals Company in the four years of the enterprise.

The initial 1950 geological planning reports for the Sino-Soviet Oil Company called for the exploration of

11 oil sites at various spots scattered around the edges of the Tarim Basin, and from 1952 to 1954, 11 surveying teams including 1 aerial surveying team were charged with pinpointing the region's oil wealth and directing future operations. In 1953, Tarim Basin geological teams surveyed over 23,000 square kilometres for the Sino-Soviet Oil Company. Yet, the high cost of operations in this isolated region, the difficult topography and the lack of transportation infrastructure slowed down the geological activities in Sinkiang's far south in 1954.

The Lisinov Li-2F aerial photography aircraft of the Soviet Air Force operating out of Dolon Air Force Base in Semipalatinsk flew hundreds of sorties over the Tarim Basin and Aksai Chin. Makeshift stopovers for refuelling were provided in Kashgar, Khotan and Shache. The entire region was minutely mapped.

All of this activity was known internationally. Unless the Government of India was both deaf and blind, the writing was clearly on the wall. It was during one of these very early aerial surveys conducted by the Soviets that they chanced upon Lake Lop Nor in the Tarim Basin as a potential site for conducting nuclear tests. It was not only an extremely remote site but the lack of population density around the long lake made it a promising site for their nuclear plans. Interestingly, the lake was situated on the old Silk Road from China to Europe. The network of routes commonly known as the 'Silk Road' resulted from an expansion of commercial and cultural exchanges between China and the Tarim Basin. Baron Ferdinand von Richthofen was a 19th-century German explorer and traveller. He identified several branches of the Silk Road across Central Asia in the 19th century.

The routes around the Taklamakan Desert in the Tarim Basin connected modern Xian in China with the western frontiers. The routes were divided around the Tarim Basin at Dunhuang, which was at the crossroads of the main route from India. The southern branch began at the Yang-Kuan Gate outside Dunhuang and followed the northern base of the Kunlun Mountains to Khotan and Kashgar. An intermediate route traversed Lop Nor and then joined the route to Khotan.

Lop Nor was not, therefore, considered a part of China proper by anyone aware of Chinese history. It was a good place, as Mao would have put it, to break wind! Further, the few inhabitants that were there were not of Han ethnicity. Mao, who was the second most ruthless practitioner of ethnopolitics in the 20th century after Stalin, considered these non-Han people around Lop Nor to be expendable in the greater glory of China's rise to power. Thus, Lop Nor became the chosen site for work to secretively start the Chinese nuclear programme. The Tarim Basin, therefore, became critical in China's scheme of things. As mentioned earlier, the primary source of freshwater for the basin is the Karakash River, which originates from Aksai Chin. Given the existence of gold and mineral deposits in and by the side of the riverbed, taking physical possession of the Karakash River became a strategic necessity for China. This was so because once Lake Lop Nor became radioactive, the eastern part of Tarim River that flowed into it would also get radioactive. Therefore, the western end of Tarim River that flows into the fertile and mineral-rich towns of Shache and Kashgar, respectively, would only remain habitable if the Karakash River flowed into it unmolested. Given Mao's vision of territorial expansion, the concern was not just about China taking physical possession of the territory in Aksai Chin through which the Karakash River flows, but it was also about the possibility of India getting evicted from her two listening posts in the region, namely Kashgar in Sinkiang and Gartok in Tibet.

The issue then was about trying to convince India by hook or by crook to voluntarily give up these two listening posts.

Chapter 12

Abdullah's Dismissal Coincides with the Birth of Joe-4

Abdullah makes the British uncomfortable

In the summer of 1951, Philby was recalled to London for interrogation on being suspected to be a Soviet spy. The Soviets, among other things, had been pressurising him to provide specific details of the four British nuclear monitoring stations in POK, namely Stowage, Beaver, Tagday and the one at Raskam village in the Shaksgam Valley. The Soviets were working very hard to have these stations closed down. The NKVD and GRU were reported to be very active in Jammu and Kashmir. However, it is unclear as to what they hoped to achieve since all the British action was in POK.

The British in all probability viewed this as an attempt to outflank their key assets in POK. They feared NKVD sabotage teams might use Jammu and Kashmir as a launchpad and destabilise the state's link with the Indian Union. If Abdullah succeeded in seceding from India with Soviet help, what implications would that have for the Gilgit Agency and NWFP? Would they then join Abdullah? The removal of Abdullah became a paramount pillar of British policy.

British overflights based on intelligence inputs confirmed the reality of the Sino-Soviet invasion of Aksai Chin. Beria was aware of the precariousness of the British position, and his objective was to destabilise Jammu and Kashmir first and then the Gilgit Agency and NWFP afterwards to compel the British to get out of the region altogether. The next logical step would be to provide a link-up between Abdullah and the Chinese.

In his seminal PhD thesis submitted to the University of Southampton, Rakesh Ankit reveals that T.G. Sanjeevi Pillai, Director of IB, wrote a top-secret note to Nehru on 5 August 1948 on the rampant presence of communists and their conspiracy to stage a coup in Kashmir. In London, there were grave concerns about the spread of communism under Abdullah's rule. By December 1948, Whitehall developed the view that Abdullah's involvement with local Indian communists and his constant contacts with the Soviets explained the steadily rising communist influence in Kashmir.

IMAGE 12.1: Freda Bedi and Baba Pyare Lal Bedi.
Source: Wikimedia Commons

Earlier in December 1950, the CIA prepared a note on communist personalities and activities in Kashmir that named B.P.L. Bedi, his wife, Freda, G.M. Sadiq, Mirza Afzal Beg, Mohiuddin

Kara and Dhanwantri. It highlighted the editorial line taken by Kashmiri publications like *Noor*, *Uplift* and *Burj*, which were allegedly funded by the Soviet and Czech embassies in New Delhi. It was especially concerned about the Bedis whom it had earlier called the 'leading light' of communism in Abdullah's administration. The Bedis were instrumental in keeping the 'inner core' of Abdullah, Bakshi and Sadiq intact. Deeply involved in the 'nationalisation' of land as well as textbooks, Baba Bedi, however, disturbed the New Delhi government as much as he was bothering Washington and London.

In January 1951, Colonel Siegfried Coblentz of the US Army and the acting chief of UN Kashmir Observers returned to Washington after serving in Kashmir there for two years and told the US State Department that the Abdullah regime—which according to Coblentz had no significant popular support and survived on threats and intimidation—represented the face of communism in the state. He was convinced that the Ministers of Communication and Education in Abdullah's Cabinet were communists. Meanwhile, the British government sent to Washington the Grafftey-Smith report on Kashmir, which the author believed was impairing the defence against communism in South Asia.

By mid-1951, the mélange of various populist economic measures forced by Abdullah, his coterie of communist advisors and his public pronouncements convinced the US State Department that the state of Jammu and Kashmir was the first port of call for both the Soviets and the Chinese communists in the subcontinent. Abdullah and his associates were believed to be in constant touch with Moscow and Beijing. Jammu and Kashmir, alongside West Asia and South East Asia, was an ideal site for Soviet intervention and communist subversion.

India's stubbornness on the Kashmir issue and its posture on international non-alignment did not help President Truman and Secretary of State Acheson gauge how long they could let the Kashmir issue remain a Commonwealth matter, especially within the context of the deteriorating British prestige over all of its former colonial possessions. One of the things holding them back was UN Representative Frank Graham's mission on Kashmir that was carried out over July, August and September 1951. Its failure, close on the heels of earlier failures under Canadian General Andrew McNaughton, US Admiral Chester Nimitz and Australian Jurist Owen Dixon, prompted the CIA to remind the State Department that the position of Kashmir will decide the final scene of the political drama over Sinkiang. However, for the British and also the Americans, the growing fear was the security of their nuclear monitoring network.

Joe-2 is born and his siblings follow

On 24 September 1951, the Soviets detonated their second nuclear device called Joe-2 in Semipalatinsk. The British monitoring stations picked up the seismic and acoustic signals. Turowicz's Halifax Squadron flew several sorties out of Chaklala and Risalpur to collect debris and validate the recordings of the monitoring stations. Although Joe-2 like its predecessor was another plutonium fission device, it was far more sophisticated because it conserved the amount of raw material needed to produce a comparable explosion. It had a 38-kiloton yield and was detonated on a tower.

More was to follow. On 18 October 1951, another signal was recorded in POK by the British stations. This was Joe-3. What was different this time was the fact that it was airdropped and used uranium as its fissionable ingredient. The same routine was followed by the Halifax Squadron, validating the recordings of the monitoring stations.

The Soviets were increasingly frustrated. In July 1951, Philby resigned from MI6 in the wake of press revelations that he was 'the third man' along with Burgess and Maclean in a Soviet spy ring. Information from the British operations in POK was drying up.

Things changed dramatically when, on 17 January 1952, Soviet Ambassador Jacob Malik made a speech in the Security Council accusing America and Britain of brazen, imperial intervention in Kashmir. This was the Soviet message to the Anglo-American alliance that their monitoring stations in POK were at risk. The American delegation to the UN interpreted this speech as a definition of the Soviet stand on several issues including support to the CPI in India's forthcoming general elections. The British added that it also reflected the Soviet desire to support an independent Kashmir under the leftist Abdullah. Abdullah's remarks to Selwyn Lloyd, the British Minister for Foreign Affairs, about his vision of independence for Jammu and Kashmir and his indifference towards the Soviet threat further confirmed that his ideas were completely contrary to those of Whitehall.

By the end of January 1952, it was clear that Malik's attempt to create greater uncertainty over Soviet intentions in Kashmir only benefitted Abdullah and the communists. The British foreign office concluded that while the Soviets were certainly not hoping to win Pakistan's sympathy, they also seemed to have overlooked that Nehru was against the communists and was concerned about internal communism in India. He also vehemently opposed the idea of an independent Kashmir. Willi Nedou, Begum Jehan Abdullah's uncle and Sheikh Abdullah's Liaison Officer in Paris, had told the British that Abdullah was seeking Soviet support for his dream. The State Department interpreted Malik's speech within the framework of the Soviet aims of laying the groundwork for an eventual communist coup in Kashmir. Further, they believed that the Soviets were clandestinely supporting the Chinese campaign in Kashgar of 'liberating' Gilgit and Ladakh. The aim was to create a circle of red in an almost unbroken line from Indo-China to Afghanistan.

On 3 October 1952, the British conducted their first nuclear test in the Indian Ocean off the Montebello Islands that lie off the western coast of Australia. It was a 25-kiloton plutonium implosion bomb. Seven years of monitoring the Soviet nuclear programme finally paid off. Later the same year, Turowicz, the leader of the Polish expatriate pilots in the PAF flying black operations into the Soviet Union in the Halifax aircraft originally from the RAF's 298 Squadron, was promoted as Wing Commander and posted as Station Commander of Chaklala.

Mookerjee's death, Abdullah's dismissal, Joe-4 detonation, all in eight weeks

In November 1952, Praja Parishad leader Prem Nath Dogra and one of his close associates Sham Lal Sharma were detained on the orders of Abdullah's interim government. In the spring of 1953, the situation in Jammu grew tense, with the Praja Parishad satyagraha. The Abdullah regime retaliated with considerable violence, dispersing crowds with police lathicharge and numerous arrests. Dr Shyama Prasad Mookerjee, a former member of Nehru's Cabinet and the founder of Bharatiya Jana Sangh, helped organise this agitation. Thereafter, in May 1953, he set out for Jammu where he proposed to investigate the situation. He was arrested at the state border by the Jammu and Kashmir state police that reported to Abdullah. Mookerjee was taken to Srinagar where he was later hospitalised due to cardiac complications. On 22 June 1953, he was administered an injection to which he was allergic, and he died the next day while under detention. Apparently, his body was not permitted to be flown to New Delhi, so his last rites were conducted in Srinagar. His demise attracted wide publicity in India where the affairs of Jammu and Kashmir always managed to become the subject of public debate. It was widely believed that he was murdered.

Abdullah's controversial role in Mookerjee's death was scrutinised with increasing anxiety by the Government of India. Who authorised the administration of the injection that allegedly killed him? Why was his detention not revoked? Who benefitted the most from his death? In hindsight, we can argue that the greatest beneficiary of Mookerjee's untimely death was the British government because it resulted in the dismissal of Abdullah from power and, with him, all his pro-Soviet fellow travellers. With him gone, the threat of a Soviet-supported coup in the Valley by Abdullah and some sort of a unilateral declaration of independence by him as a consequence was eliminated. Such action by Abdullah could have resulted in the collapse of other dominoes like Hunza and Chitral, and the creation of an independent Soviet-supported state in the region, which would have been inimical to British interests.

There was also the issue of TASS correspondent N. Pastukhov's visits to Srinagar, which caused concern in the IB. Did Pastukhov wear a second hat? Was he actually an NKVD/GRU officer working under TASS cover? Was Pastukhov the 'puppeteer' in the planned Soviet-supported coup by Abdullah? Were these emerging alignments a clear and present danger to both the British and the Indian governments? The Director of IB B.N. Mullick believed that Mookerjee's death, whatever its causes, was the last straw and demanded intervention. Karan Singh flew to New Delhi in the third week of July 1953 to seek instructions from Nehru. Thereafter, on his return to Srinagar, Singh and D.P. Dhar, a young member of Abdullah's administration, teamed up with Abdullah's deputy Bakshi Ghulam Mohammed and decided to bring the crisis to an end by removing Abdullah from power.

Major B.S. Bajwa and ADC to the Sadr-e-Riyasat Karan Singh, accompanied by a police party, were sent to Gulmarg to arrest Abdullah in the early hours of the morning on 9 August 1953. Abdullah and his wife were driven out to Udhampur and detained at the Tara Niwas guest house. Karan Singh, thereafter, swore in Ghulam Mohammed to replace Abdullah. The Indian Army and allied security forces in the state were placed on high alert and various other security measures, including press censorship, were announced. Under the new administration of Ghulam Mohammed and with the fall of Abdullah, the Praja Parishad agitation in Jammu disappeared. The death of Mookerjee thus appeared to have been avenged. The arrest and detention of Abdullah provided the Government of India quite a few years of relative calm.

Barely three days later, on 12 August 1953, the Soviets detonated Joe-4 at the Semipalatinsk test site. It yielded roughly 400 kilotons of TNT. The explosion took place on a tower; the purpose of this was to reduce the fallout hazard, which would be created as a result of the explosion. The test vaporised the steel tower and left a massive crater in its place. The area surrounding the crater was covered in a 'yellow lumpy glass' that became thinner from the epicentre.

Abdullah's arrest and the dismissal of his administration also brought immense relief to the British. The discovery of the Joe-4 detonation had to be studied in detail. The British could now focus on that without the fear of being outflanked by the Soviets even at their tail.

Abdullah had dug his own grave. Did the Soviets lead him up the garden path only to pull back when they realised the limitations of Sadiq and Baba Bedi in helping Abdullah achieve his objective of a Moscow-supported independent Kashmir? Or was a likely Soviet-supported coup by Abdullah barely nipped in the bud by the untimely demise of Mookerjee? Was Abdullah even aware of what medication was administered and planned for Mookerjee? Were the statements of the consulting and administering doctors on why Mookerjee was injected with the fatal drug ever recorded? Was an honest post-mortem and inquest denied because there was a conspiracy to murder Mookerjee? Was Nehru's use of the excuse of Mookerjee's custodial death to dismiss Abdullah's government really a way of helping the British? Abdullah's arrest certainly doused the momentum that was being generated to take the Valley of Kashmir 'independent' under a red flag.

Or was this Mullick's super move to manipulate Nehru to achieve British ends?

However, the move to oust Abdullah from power also swept aside the demand to conduct an inquest into the real reasons for Mookerjee's questionable death in custody.

Unfortunately, we will never really know the truth.

POSTSCRIPT

On 29 April 1954, India and China signed the Panchsheel Agreement on peaceful coexistence. By this agreement, India surrendered her traditional rights in Tibet and also shut down her Consulates in Lhasa and Kashgar in Sinkiang. By signing this agreement, India accepted and condoned China's usurpation of a vast swathe of her territory in the Aksai Chin region of Jammu and Kashmir and also acquiesced to the organised loot of her mineral resources in Aksai Chin by the Soviet Union and China.

On Sunday 21 November 1954, Welsh died of a heart attack.

On 21 September 1955, the Soviet Union commissioned a new nuclear test site on the arctic island of Novaya Zemlya by detonating Joe-17, the 17th Soviet nuclear explosion.

On 22 November 1955, Joe-19 was detonated in Semipalatinsk. This was a 'monster' bomb and was an airburst explosion with a yield of 1.6 megatons, more than 100 times the yield of the Hiroshima bomb. The first signal received from the detonation anywhere in the world was at the British station called Stowage in the Gilgit Agency in POK. This was quickly followed by the receipt of signals at Beaver, Tagday and Raskam monitoring stations also in POK. Acoustic data indicated a higher yield of 1.7 megatons. Days later, radiochemical analysis confirmed that the test was of a bomb dropped from an aircraft in flight. In all probability, it was a two-stage hydrogen bomb. CIA reports indicated that the US was only 18 months ahead of the Soviets in the nuclear race. The British and American intelligence discovered that after Joe-19, all high-yield Soviet tests were set to be conducted off Nova Zemlya. Clearly, the four monitoring stations in POK were no longer going to be the prima donnas that they had been since their inception in 1946.

On 23 March 1956, Pakistan ceased to be a British Dominion.

On 31 December 1956, Britain finally withdrew its military forces from the Indian subcontinent. When Pakistan was established on 14 August 1947, the RAF maintained its presence in the country, sharing facilities in Mauripur near Karachi with the then-new RPAF. As a staging post, Mauripur continued as a strategic link between the UK, Far East and Australia. After 31 December 1947, Mauripur was redesignated as the RAF Staff of HQ for the British forces in Pakistan. This HQ was composed of an integrated Army and RAF staff then under the command of Group Captain Denis Hensley Fulton Barnett. Right through until the end of 1956, hundreds of aircraft of various nations staged through, the most regular visitors being Avro Hastings of RAF Transport Command on their way to and from the British nuclear test site in Australia. Mauripur was also an emergency backup airfield for Karachi Airport. Mauripur staging post closed on 31 December 1956, when operations were transferred to RAF Gan. It holds the distinction of being the last operational RAF airfield on the Indian subcontinent to close operations.

On 19 September 1960, Prime Minister Nehru of India and President Ayub Khan of Pakistan signed the Indus Waters Treaty regarding the distribution of the waters of the six rivers of the Indus water system. This treaty superseded the Inter-Dominion Accord of 4 May 1948, whereby river water was released to Pakistan by India. The treaty gave the lion's share of the waters of the Indus water system to Pakistan. By signing this treaty, India acquiesced to the illegal usurpation and control of vast parts of Jammu and Kashmir by Pakistan since 1947.

Neither Pakistan nor China has ever been satisfied by India's accommodation of their aggression. This aggression has continued unabated till 2021 with no end in sight.

REFERENCES

Aldrich, Richard J. 1998. 'Britain's Secret Intelligence Service in Asia During the Second World War.' *Modern Asian Studies* 32, No. 1. Cambridge, UK: Cambridge University Press.

Ahmad, Omair https://thewire.in/books/nambiar-secret-life

Anonymous. 2007. 'Brief Life Sketch of Air Commodore Wladyslaw Turowicz of Pakistan Air Force.' *Pakistani Aviation Forum*.

Balachandran, Vappala https://caravanmagazine.in/vantage/acn-nambiar-nehru-indira-bose-ambassador

Bandyopadhyay, Sekhar. 2014. *From Plassey to Partition and After: A History of Modern India*. Calcutta: Orient Longman.

Barker, Ralph. 1969. *Aviator Extraordinary: The Sidney Cotton Story*. London: Chatto & Windus.

Baumer, Christoph. 2018. *The History of Central Asia: The Age of Decline and Revival*. London: I.B. Tauris.

Beg, Sofia. 'Remembering Burhan ud Din.' Chitral News (13 August 2018).

Benson, Linda K. and Ingvar Svanberg. 1998. *China's Last Nomads: The History and Culture of China's Kazaks*. New York: M.E. Sharpe.

Bogle, Lori Lyn. 2001. *The Cold War: Hot Wars of the Cold War*. New York: Routledge.

Bose, Arun Coomer. 1971. *The Indian Revolutionaries and the Bolsheviks: Their Early Contacts, 1918–1922*. New Delhi: National Archives of India.

Bowyer, Michael J.F. and John D.R. Rawlings. 1979. *Squadron Codes: 1937–56*. Cambridge, UK: Patrick Stephens.

Chakrabarty, Bidyut. 2014. *Communism in India: Events, Processes & Ideologies*. New Delhi: Oxford University Press.

Cheema, Aamir Mushtaq. 2018. *An Illustrated History of the Chitral Scouts (1903–2014)*. New York: Ishi Press International.

Chitaley, D.V. 1946. *All India Reporter*. Nagpur: All India Reporter Pvt. Ltd.

Clubb, O.E. 1971. *China and Russia: The Great Game*. New York: Columbia University Press.

Departure of Air Marshal H.S.P. Walmsley (PDF). *Press Information Bureau of India Archive*. 13 November 1947.

Dickens, Mark. 1990. 'The Soviets in Xinjiang, 1911–1949.' Undergrad Paper. University of Alberta, Alberta. https://www.academia.edu/398262/The_Soviets_In_Xinjiang

Dillon, Michael. 2017. *Xinjiang and the Expansion of Chinese Communist Power*. Oxford: Routledge.

File No. 87011p1692 PoI declassified from the Indian Prime Minister's Office.

Flowerday, Julie. 2019. 'Identity Matters: Hunza and the Hidden Text of Britain and China.' *South Asian History and Culture* 10, No. 1.

Goodman, Michael S. 2007. *Spying on the Nuclear Bear: Anglo-American Intelligence and the Soviet Bomb*. Stanford: Stanford University Press.

Goodman, Michael S. 2016. 'MI6's Atomic Man: The Rise and Fall of Commander Eric Welsh.' *War in History* 23, No. 1. London: SAGE Publishing.

Gup, Ted. 2001. *The Book of Honor: The Secret Lives and Deaths of CIA Operatives*. New York: Anchor.

Hajari, Nisid. 2015. *Midnight's Furies: The Deadly Legacy of India's Partition*. New York: Mariner Books.

Harper, Tim. 2020. *Underground Asia: Global Revolutionaries and the Assault on Empire*. Cambridge, Massachusetts: Harvard University Press.

Hingorani, Aman M. 2017. *Unravelling the Kashmir Knot*. New Delhi: SAGE Publishing.

Hodson, H.V. 2004. *The Great Divide: Britain–India–Pakistan*. Pakistan: Oxford University Press.

Hyatt, Ishrat. Braveheart. *Facebook*. 28 February 2020.

James, L (1997), Raj, the Making and Unmaking of British India, London: Abacus Before Keegan, John (ed). 1991.

Keegan, John (ed). 1991. *Churchill's Generals*. London: Cassell.

Kurlander, Eric "Hitler's Monsters" by Kurlander and Published by Yale University Press after Churchill's Generals. London: Cassell

Laird, Thomas. 2003. *Into Tibet: The CIA's First Atomic Spy and His Secret Expedition to Lhasa*. New York: Grove Press.

Lamb, Alastair. 1994. *Birth of a Tragedy: Kashmir 1947*. Hertingfordbury: Roxford Books.

Louro, Michele L. "Comrades against Imperialism: Nehru, India, and Interwar Internationalism by Cambridge University Press, U.K.

Maitra, K. 1978. 'Comintern, Roy and the Possibility of an Armed Revolution in India.' *Proceedings of the Indian History Congress* 39, No. II. New Delhi: Indian History Congress.

Mathur, B.P. https://mainstreamweekly.net/article11647.html

Malhotra, Iqbal Chand. https://openthemagazine.com/columns/guest-column/red-shadow-behind-subhas-chandra-bose/

Malhotra, Iqbal Chand. 2020. *Red Fear: The China Threat*. New Delhi: Bloomsbury.

Malhotra, Iqbal Chand and Maroof Raza. 2021. *Kashmir's Untold Story: Declassified*. New Delhi: Bloomsbury.

Mead, Richard. 2007. *Churchill's Lions: A Biographical Guide to the Key British Generals of World War II*. Stroud: Spellmount.

Middleton, Robert. 2019. 'The Russians in the Great Game.' Research Paper. Bishkek: Cultural Heritage and Humanities Unit, University of Central Asia.

Majumdar, Sisir K. (1997), "http://www.revolutionarydemocracy.org/rdv7n1/Bose.htm" "Subhas Chandra Bose in Nazi Germany", South Asia Forum Quarterly, Chery Chase, Maryland, 10 (1), retrieved 6 February 2016

Morrison, Alexander. 2020. *The Russian Conquest of Central Asia: A Study in Imperial Expansion, 1814–1914*. Cambridge, UK: Cambridge University Press.

Osborn, Patrick. 2000. *Operation Pike: Britain Versus the Soviet Union, 1939–1941*. Santa Barbara, CA: Greenwood Publishing.

PTI https://economictimes.indiatimes.com/magazines/panache/a-c-n-nambiar-netaji-subhash-chandra-bose-deputy-jawaharlal-nehru-aide-was-soviet-spy-reveal-british-docs/articleshow/44931929.cms

Pakistan Defence. 'INA and Bur-han-uddin of Chitral', 10 January 2016. https://cbkwgl.wordpress.com/2015/11/06/burhan-ud-din-of-chitral/

Pondrom, L.G. 2018. *The Soviet Atomic Project: How the Soviet Union Obtained the Atomic Bomb*. Nashville: Acuff Rose Publications.

Press Communiqué (PDF). *Press Information Bureau of India Archive.* 10 November 1947. https://archive.pib.gov.in/archive/ArchiveSecondPhase/DEFENCE/1947-AUG-DEC-DEFENCE/PDF/DEF-1947-11-10_042.pdf

Press Communiqué (PDF). *Press Information Bureau of India Archive.* 1 December 1947. https://archive.pib.gov.in/archive/ArchiveSecondPhase/DEFENCE/1947-AUG-DEC-DEFENCE/PDF/DEF-1947-11-29_091.pdf

Press Note (PDF). *Press Information Bureau of India Archive.* 1 August 1947. https://archive.pib.gov.in/archive/ArchiveSecondPhase/DEFENCE/1947-JULY-DEC-MIN-OF-DEFENCE/PDF/DEF-1947-08-01_332.pdf

Press Note (PDF). *Press Information Bureau of India Archive.* 22 October 1947. https://archive.pib.gov.in/archive/ArchiveSecondPhase/DEFENCE/1947-AUG-DEC-DEFENCE/PDF/DEF-1947-10-22_023.pdf

Press Report (PDF). *Press Information Bureau of India Archive.* 15 November 1947. https://archive.pib.gov.in/archive/ArchiveSecondPhase/DEFENCE/1947-AUG-DEC-DEFENCE/PDF/DEF-1947-11-15_050.pdf

Rawlings, John D.R. 1982. *Coastal, Support and Special Squadrons of the RAF and their Aircraft.* London: Jane's Publishing.

Roy, Purabi. 2011. *The Search for Netaji: New Findings.* New Delhi: Purple Peacocks.

Sarila, Narendra Singh. 2009. *The Shadow of the Great Game: The Untold Story of India's Partition.* New Delhi: HarperCollins.

Shamberg, Vladimir. 2001. *The Soviet Atomic Bomb.* Colorado Springs: USAF Academy.

Slim, Field Marshal William. 1956. *Defeat into Victory.* London: Cassell.

Smith, Constance Babington. 2004. *Evidence in Camera: The Story of Photographic Intelligence in the Second World War.* Stroud, UK: Sutton Publishing.

Smith, Timothy. 2014. *Vietnam and the Unravelling of Empire: General Gracey in Asia 1942–1951.* London: Palgrave.

Snedden, Christopher. 2015. *Understanding Kashmir and Kashmiris.* London: C. Hurst & Co.

Surjeet, Harkishan Singh. 1998. *March of the Communist Movement in India: An Introduction to the Documents of the History of the Communist Movement in India.* Calcutta: National Book Agency.

Talwar, Bhagat Ram (1976), HYPERLINK "https://books.google.com/books?id=l8gBAAAAMAAJ&q=+great+escape" The Talwar's of Pathan Land and Subhas Chandra's Great Escape, People's Publishing House, HYPERLINK "https://en.wikipedia.org/wiki/ISBN_(identifier)"ISBN HYPERLINK "https://en.wikipedia.org/wiki/Special:BookSources/978-0-88386-848-5"978-0-88386-848-5

Tomlinson, B.R. 1976. *The Indian National Congress and the Raj, 1929–1942: The Penultimate Phase*. UK: Palgrave Macmillan.

Thomson, Mike (23 September 2004), HYPERLINK "http://news.bbc.co.uk/1/hi/3684288.stm" Hitler's secret Indian army, HYPERLINK "https://en.wikipedia.org/wiki/BBC_News"BBC News

Warner, Philip. 1982. *Auchinleck: The Lonely Soldier*. London: Sphere Books.

Watson, Jeff. 2004. *Sidney Cotton: The Last Plane Out of Berlin*. Sydney: Hodder Headline Australia.

Whistler, Lashmer Gordon. 'Last British Unit to Leave India on February 28—General Whistler's Address to Senior Officers.' *Press Information Bureau of India Archive*. 18 February 1948.

Willmott, H.P. 2010. *The Last Century of Sea Power (Volume 2): From Washington to Tokyo, 1922–1945*. Bloomington: Indiana University Press.

Willmott, Peter. 2016. *The Papers of Air Marshal Sir Thomas Elmhirst*. Cambridge, UK: Janus Book Publishing.

Zachariah, Benjamin https://www.researchgate.net/publication/283581631_Indian_political_activities_in_Germany_1914-1945 after Willmott, Peter.

INDEX

ABOUT THE AUTHOR

Iqbal Chand Malhotra has produced over five hundred hours of programming telecasts worldwide. He has directed four internationally acclaimed, award-winning feature documentaries. He is a member of the International Academy of Television Arts and Sciences and has served for several years on the panel of jurors for the International Emmy Awards. Malhotra is the author of *Red Fear: The China Threat* and *The Bomb, the Bank, the Mullah and the Poppies: A Tale of Deception* and co-author of *Kashmir's Untold Story: Declassified* all published by Bloomsbury India. He is Chairman and Producer, AIM Television, New Delhi.